Advance Praise for *Tales from the Sustainable Underground*

Food is too fundamental, and food security too critical to be bound by a law built to serve corporations and agribusiness. A growing movement based on the civil right to good, save food is standing outside the law — and pointing up the law's injustice. This is an important and necessary book about a resistance movement as fundamental as any social justice movement in history.

> — Sharon Astyk, writer (scienceblogs.com/casaubonsbook), farmer and author of *Depletion and Abundance, Independence Days* and *Making Home* (sharonastyk.com)

Off-grid, offbeat, but right on target, Stephen Hren's glimpse into the lives of those making viable choices at the fringes of society is a real revelation. Hren's accounts of neo-primitivists, green anarchists, urban squatters and other pioneers working towards a sustainable future is consistently inspiring and informative.

> — Richard Freudenberger, Publisher, *BackHome* Magazine

In *Tales from the Sustainable Underground*, Stephen Hren proves that plenty of Americans are ready to take back their country — one plot of land at a time, if necessary. Through personal insight and engaging interviews with sustainable citizens, Hren masterfully spins a cross-country tale about the "doers" who are helping to bring sustainability out of the shadows and usher in a return of this country's "can-do" attitude.

> — Roger Sipe, Editor, *Urban Farm* magazine

Stephen Hren stitches together stories about the option open to each of us faced with resource depletion, energy descent and climate change— doing things differently even if it is against the law or socially unpopular. This book will inspire you to explore that option. Thanks to Hren for being brave enough to write it.

> — Aaron Newton, farmer, activist, outlaw chicken raiser and co-author of *A Nation of Farmers*

Most activists and counter culture types have their ups and downs, sometimes I feel less hopeful and then... along comes a book like this... WOW! *Tales From The Sustainable Underground* is an amazing, magical tapestry of a multitude of different people's "lifestyle" choices. Each story takes you deeper into hearts and minds of others who are willing to take the risk of not belonging in a culture that craves sameness while marketing it and fetishizing it as "individuality." This book is inspiring, informative, educational, nourishing and uplifting, a must-read for anyone who wants to make a difference in the world!

— Dirk Becker, Activist, Farmer, Educator, Public Speaker
and Urban Farming Local Food Advocate

TALES FROM THE

Sustainable Underground

TALES FROM THE
Sustainable
Underground

A WILD JOURNEY WITH PEOPLE
WHO CARE MORE ABOUT THE PLANET
THAN THE LAW

Stephen Hren

NEW SOCIETY PUBLISHERS

Printed in Canada. First printing September 2011.
Paperback ISBN: 978-0-86571-687-2
eISBN: 978-1-55092-487-9

Inquiries regarding requests to reprint all or part of *Tales from the
Sustainable Underground* should be addressed to New Society Publishers
at the address below.

To order directly from the publishers, please call toll-free (North America)
1-800-567-6772, or order online at www.newsociety.com

Any other inquiries can be directed by mail to:

New Society Publishers
P.O. Box 189, Gabriola Island, BC V0R 1X0, Canada
(250) 247-9737

New Society Publishers' mission is to publish books that contribute in fundamental
ways to building an ecologically sustainable and just society, and to do so with the
least possible impact on the environment, in a manner that models this vision. We
are committed to doing this not just through education, but through action. The
interior pages of our bound books are printed on Forest Stewardship Council® acid-
free paper that is **100% post-consumer recycled** (100% old growth forest-free),
processed chlorine free, and printed with vegetable-based, low-VOC inks, with
covers produced using FSC® stock. New Society also works to reduce its carbon
footprint, and purchases carbon offsets based on an annual audit to ensure a carbon
neutral footprint. For further information, or to browse our full list of books and
purchase securely, visit our website at: www.newsociety.com

LIBRARY AND ARCHIVES CANADA CATALOGUING IN PUBLICATION

Hren, Stephen, 1974–
Tales from the sustainable underground : a wild journey with people who care
more about the planet than the law / Stephen Hren.

Includes index.
ISBN 978-0-86571-687-2

1. Environmentalists — Biography. 2. Sustainable living.
3. Green movement. I. Title.

GE55.H74 2011   333.72092'2   C2011-905174-5

NEW SOCIETY PUBLISHERS
www.newsociety.com

To the doers.

—

"To live outside the law you must be honest."
—Bob Dylan

Contents

Foreword

by Lyle Estill

When I first caught wind of *Sustainable Underground* I was jazzed. I thought of all the laws that have been written in support of the status quo, and of all the nights people in the sustainability movement have spent sweating over breaking them. I felt it was a story aching to be told.

When it was kicked around by the publishing industry, I encouraged Stephen to stick with it. I'm glad he did, because it became a wonderful read.

I found myself laughing out loud at the sight of Stephen with his high-end coffee maker at the campsite of the primitive anarchists — deprived of his morning caffeine fix for lack of fire lighting skills. And I found myself heartbroken to read of the collapse of a Texas collective based on organizational deficiencies.

Stephen brings his background, his humility, and his baggage to the book. In doing so he adds a delightful personal level which helps embellish the facts. Those who know Stephen know that he lives low on the carbon consumption totem pole, with intention. And while he is an inspiration to those who know him, he is often treated as a well-heeled novice by some of the characters in this book.

I was in Paris when Stephen's email arrived — asking for a foreword "by yesterday." I immediately dropped my Hemmingway and Miller to give *Sustainable Underground* a read. As soon as I delved into the manuscript I was visited by Jean Paul Sartre who insisted, "existence precedes essence."

Can a lowly building inspector know the essence of a completed cob house before such a thing exists? Possibly not. Sartre was right, Stephen had offered up existential proof, and all was well.

To write this book Stephen embarked on a series of wild journeys around America to not only visit, but also to probe those activists, and doers who are reshaping our society's landscape into something that might sustain human life on this garden planet.

Sometimes flaunting the law, sometimes hiding from it, and sometimes ignoring it completely, the real life characters in *Sustainable Underground* are all pushing the envelope of societal change.

I feel it is a daring book. When it comes to the "War on Drugs," for instance, Stephen not only delves into the issue, but also makes himself known as a partisan with the underdog side. I admire that courage. It makes me want to join the fight, rather than staying silent, with my stash kept in my refrigerator door.

With its many stories and interconnections; from art to primitive anarchism to urban renewal, *Sustainable Underground* draws on everything from Faulkner to neighborhood activists. In doing so it engenders a certain faith that perhaps our species is capable of a wholesale change that might empower and sustain us all.

I suppose the notion of "faith" might indicate that Sartre had it wrong. *Sustainable Underground* calls on the reader to find the *essence*, of things before those things can be brought into existence.

Either way the book provides us with a necessary start point where we can forget about the law and the current order of things so that we can think differently about the world we inhabit, and reshape it in a way that allows us to thrive within those limits which are imposed upon us by nature.

Lyle Estill has been taking chances with the law and disrupting the status quo since he started making fuel with Piedmont Biofuels in 2002. He is the the publisher of Energy Blog, and author of Biodiesel Power, Small is Possible *and* Industrial Evolution. *LyleEstill.com*

Introduction

Plopping that first pile of mud onto the foundation felt revolutionary...and illegal. After years of research, saving money and living in a
yurt, my former wife and I were starting out building our own home,
a place we intended (at least at the time!) to live the rest of our lives.
Yet our building permit described a much more conventional home, a
stick-built square cabin that any inspector would recognize as familiar,
not the round cob home we were now building.

After an initial frenzy of finding beautiful and affordable land,
making the time commitments to build, getting our building permits
and septic and well and drawing on what turned out to be woefully
inadequate building skills, we'd changed our minds from the square
cabin to a monolithic dome, managed to get a foundation poured, and
then run out of money. So we took the last chunk of change, built a
yurt and moved in. We thought we needed space, so we made it big,
perhaps the biggest yurt in the world: 32 feet in diameter. We lived in
it, even though it baked in the summer and held as much heat as worn
out lingerie in the winter. We worked, we finished college, we moved
away for a year and then the whole thing fell down in a massive two-
foot snow storm.

We were in Mali at the time, visiting a friend in the Peace Corps.
It was just after the new millennium started, January 2000. We visited
amazing places, like Djenne, where there was a seven-story mosque
built out of earth, and countless other homes built out of the land
they sat on. These were beautiful, simple homes, small but accom-
modating, decorated with love and attention, cool during the day and
warm at night. Meantime, we ran into some fellow travelers from our
neck of the woods, and heard tell of the snow storm back home, feet

of snow and then more ice on top of it, rare indeed for us southerners. Tentatively, we began to express doubts about our not so little yurt in the woods and if it could have withstood such an onslaught.

There were still weeks of traveling. Finally we made it back to North Carolina, got in the car and made the drive out. As we crested the hill of our property, we should have had a good view of our 14-foot-tall yurt through the bare trees. Yet we saw nothing. And so we knew. We parked and walked down the hill to find a swimming pool with an outline of our stuff on the bottom. The conical top section of the yurt had collapsed, but the cylindrical lattice-work bottom portion had held. The result was that the canvas that had made up the top was now a pool liner, with our bed, stereo, kitchen, etc. now underneath thousands of gallons of water. It was almost too funny to be upsetting, and we had been trying to figure out a way to get the mammoth yurt down without killing ourselves anyways. In our year away of work we had saved up money, and we were ready to start again and try to do things right.

After the amazing buildings we'd seen on our travels, the square conventionally-framed cabin described in our building plans looked downright pathetic and unappealing. Even the monolithic dome we'd poured the foundation for seemed too technocentric and energy intensive. What to do? Conveniently, our inherent cheapness had saddled us with a large pile of earth just downhill from our building site. The folks who'd dug out the foundation had offered to haul it away for 50 bucks or so, but we told them to just dump it down there at the bottom. We'd kind of regretted the decision, until now. Here was a gigantic pile of red clay, waiting for a purpose. After some dawdling, we decided to go for it. There was some vague talk of cob on the nascent Internet, and we ordered a lightly worded how-to book by Becky Bee. We made some test bricks. We found a good mix. We made a small model out of construction paper of the building we intended to build. And then we mixed up a batch of cob with our bare feet on a torn section of collapsed yurt canvas and plopped it on our foundation.

Without, of course, bothering to change our building permit. Which brings me to the subject of this book. Because at that moment, both of us became part of something that we had no idea existed. With that first plop of mud onto that foundation, we had entered the Sustainable Underground.

There was the revolutionary sixties that petered out in the seventies, followed by the wasteland of the eighties. Then starting in the early nineties something started to happen in North America. People throughout the land started to figure out that the way we were living was unsustainable. To wit, it could not be sustained. Some said to themselves, why live a life that cannot be sustained? It almost goes against the meaning of the word "life" itself. Some people wrote about this unsustainability problem, some folks talked to politicians about it, some talked to their spouses about it over dinner. But some folks just went out and *did* stuff. And they didn't ask permission first. Because why should you have to ask permission to do something that's right? Why should you have to ask permission to build a home out of the materials available right on your own land? Why should you have to ask permission to run your home off sunlight? Who has the right to outlaw compost? Why should you need permission to use an abandoned and decaying building? Who says you can't make giant sculpture on your property? What ever made people think they can make a plant illegal? What were they thinking when they said you can't cook food in your own kitchen and feed your neighbor?

What happened to some of these doers is what happened to us. We got busted. After three years of hard labor, we finished our cob home and moved in. It turned out great, but there was always that nagging feeling that we were living in a home that was illegal. It's hard to hide a house. It's not like a quarter-bag of pot that you can squirrel away in your underwear drawer. It's out there. We were still connected to the utility with a temporary electric pole, but we were working towards an off-grid solar electric system and hoped to get the grid turned off soon. But the world was moving too fast for us. Satellite images of our property unmistakably revealed an odd round building that caught the eye of our county tax assessor. And of course he was obliged to tell the county inspector about our illegal home.

To anyone who's ever lived underground (i.e., hiding from the law), there's always that fear of the dreadful moment of getting caught. Ours happened when I had just got back from work late in the afternoon. I parked at the top of the hill and hopped out of the car to take a leak. My relief was temporary, because I soon noticed a suspicious white truck coming from the direction of our cob home. The man rolled down his window and said, "I've got a report of some folks living in an uninspected building on this property. You know anything about it?" Startled out of my urinary reverie, I made a split second decision that would change the course of my life and my former wife's. I told the truth. "Uh, yeah, that would be me."

And then something very unexpected happened. A little sliver of trust developed between me and that public official, the "Man" and the "squatter." The man in the truck replied, "I need you to come down to my office so we can talk about this matter. Give me a call by the end of the week." He handed over his card, and then said, "You can go back to taking your piss now," and drove off.

Was this the end? Was our beloved cob home about to be bulldozed by men who drove around in white trucks? It turns out there was an alternate ending. The inspector allowed us to prove to him that not only was our cob home strong and safe enough to be legal, but that our solar electric system was legitimate, too. After some improvements, and a year or so of back and forth, we got our Certificate of Occupancy. Our solar cob home was legal! What had started out as revolutionary just five years before was now aboveboard, legit. And that meant we weren't afraid to show our home to other people and teach them about natural building and solar electricity. They could use our home as a precedent for creating similar systems on their own property.

It didn't take long after that to start hearing about lots of other cool stuff going on around North Carolina. A few counties over, crazy folks were huddled over pieced-together piping and antique solar water heaters, turning waste veggie oil into biodiesel and driving ancient Mercedes around. Folks up in the mountains were building an eco-village of small homes built of straw and discarded windows on a dead end road that entered another county and where inspectors rarely roamed. My artist friend Matt had bought property up in the Catskills of New York and was building giant inhabitable sculptures made of twigs, rocks and detritus from nearby New York City. And each person seemed to know about at least one other group or person doing something equally crazy and daring and who were determined to not just drop out of civilization, because that just doesn't work anymore with globalized everything, especially problems like global climate disruption. They were determined to change the very fabric of society from the bottom up. I wanted to meet them all!

Of course I haven't met them all. Hopefully, that's not even possible because of the sheer number of awesome folks experimenting across the land. But I did meet some amazing and incredibly inspiring people with some fantastic stories. Originally, I thought this book would be about activists dedicated to sustainability who think it's easier to ask forgiveness than ask permission. To some extent, the varied group of folks I met on my big summertime journey in 2010 did consider themselves activists, but these were in the minority and honestly, almost no one I met seemed the least bit contrite. Mostly they're just doing what they believe is right to make the world a sane and livable place, and any effect they've had, or will have, on the law of the land is accidental. But whether challenging the law is what they set out to do or not, there's no denying that is what they're doing, and we all benefit from their courage and hard work.

There are laws that are worth having and ones that aren't, and the well-being of our society depends on a constant process of trying to increase the number of good ones and reduce the number of bad ones. When you come across a bad law and want to change it, there are two ways to go about it. There's the conventional way of going down to city hall or the county commissioners or contacting your representative and trying to get them to sponsor a bill or give them a signed petition of concerned citizens. Which is a great thing to do. But a great deal of what makes for a sustainable life are functioning systems that need to exist in the first place for conventionally minded folks like a representative to understand that they do work. Systems like a home built out of natural materials, or an effective means of composting human waste or a small community-supported kitchen run out of a neighborhood home. Asking for permission to create something that the legislator can't conceive of — let alone it working properly — is very unlikely to meet with any success. You have to have the thing before it can become legal, but you can't have it without building it or doing it first. And the folks I met on my journey are doing just that.

1

Detroit

DETROIT WAS ACTUALLY the last stop I made on my big round-the-country journey looking for some answers — or at least some insightful questions and interesting stories — on what it's going to take to change the law of the land so that a sustainable life is even potentially legal, much less standard practice. But the more I thought about the place, the more iconic it seemed as a prime example of where we went wrong, and also as a Petri dish of what could change for the better. So it makes sense to start with this most intriguing of metropolises.

Detroit is dying; Detroit is pulsating with life. Both are true, and the place is, at least on a few levels, undergoing a metamorphosis from a corporate car town to a thriving hub of grassroots artistic and re-generative experimentation. While broad avenues built for massive car traffic now lay barely used with plastic bags caught in dead weeds growing through cracks in the pavement, the residents of the city are reinventing themselves by growing their own food on abandoned land, running vegan restaurants out of their foreclosed homes and elaborately decorating nearby abandoned buildings to preserve them and scare away the crackheads.

Detroit is corrupt, almost utterly so. While I was there, the spec-ter of ex-mayor Kwame Kilpatrick's felony charges for paying nine million dollars of public funds to police officers to try and cover up an extramarital affair hung over the city, as did a multitude of other scandals including bribery and the embezzlement of educational funds involving a police chief and several former city council members. Over its two-hundred-year existence, the city has a long history of piling up laws on top of laws, many passed with special interests in mind rather than the welfare of the public. It seemed like whoever I spoke with said that what they were doing was illegal for some reason or another, in violation of some relic of a statute that was somewhat contradicted by another statute under a different department.

Laws can have two different purposes. They can protect the welfare of the less powerful by holding those with more power accountable. Or they can reinforce the privilege, Latin for "private law," of the elite and keep the little guy from achieving any independence. Often it is the case that laws that start out with the purpose of, or at least the pretense of, promoting the former end up over time turning into the latter. Power, it seems, is the most addictive thing on earth. No amount of it is satisfying. The people I met in this dynamic city, and all across the country, were mostly violating laws that started out as reasonable but ended up being used as a source of privilege and corruption. The motivations of the amazingly diverse group of folks I met who were challenging laws across the land were remarkably consistent, a mix of a longing for more personal independence and a desire to bring their lives and communities back into the cycle of life. It was a great inspiration to see how consistently these two goals were achieved by the same actions.

Part of what makes Detroit so interesting as a jumping off point is how unsustainably it grew after 1900, especially as the advent of the automobile industry transformed the town into the Motor City. Detroit was one of the first cities to embrace the automobile on a large scale, with Henry Ford's five-dollars-a-day wage given much of the credit for developing a manufacturing middle class capable of affording this luxury. All technology is a double-edged sword, and whatever conveniences it provides come at the cost of more dependencies. The car culture that swallowed Detroit's city planning is an excellent example of this. The rampant suburbanization that didn't severely affect many cities until after World War II was already evident in 1920's Detroit. Many main thoroughfares are four or five lanes wide, even in the older parts of town. Trying to cross these mammoth and decaying boulevards on foot feels foolhardy, and the fear of the light changing before you're anywhere near the other side is constant. Getting around without a car, unlike in neighboring midwestern cities like Milwaukee and Chicago, is unimaginable to a newcomer like myself.

Detroit continued its road-building binge after World War II, steamrolling older neighborhoods to make way for a bevy of interstates to ferry fearful whites out to the burbs from downtown. It worked. And then these urban refugees decided they would simply build their businesses out where they lived, especially after the Twelfth Street riot raged for five days in the summer of 1967 leaving 43 dead. Next, the oil spikes of the 1970s came and put massive dents in the auto industry. By the turn of the millennium, large swaths of the city had been abandoned and burned to the ground. Finding a grocery store became close to impossible for many urban residents.

All of this puts Detroit at the forefront of dealing with issues that are likely to plague the rest of the nation, and potentially the world, this century. Dwindling fossil fuel supplies will likely make much of the suburbs in their current form uninhabitable. Importing food long distances is likewise suspect. Archaic and poorly applied laws, relics of the days of cheap fossil fuels and ignorance of global climate disruption, hinder and exasperate attempts to retrofit existing infrastructure for sustainability. Every city faces the prospect of lower populations, so the paradigm of paying for existing infrastructure with revenue from new growth is suspect everywhere. Most fundamentally, relying on a culture that attempts to derive its satisfaction from ever-increasing quantities of material goods rather than a deep connection with nature, community and personal spirituality is no longer possible for most folks in Detroit. The material economy has been decreasing for decades.

While responding with fear and dread to these disturbing phenomena is understandable, many Detroiters have also come to understand that relying on a fix from the powers that be is foolhardy at best. Mistrust of the law's benevolence has combined with an ingrained DIY ethic to get folks out from in front of their TVs and computers and trying to do stuff to improve their lives and communities, regardless of the law or the outdated mores of their neighbors.

To understand whether changing any particular law will allow for a more profound flourishing of sustainability, it helps to start off with at least a cursory examination of the foundations of our culture and to test the bedrock upon which it rests. I found a great forum for exploring these deeper questions when I showed up at Dabl's and Perette's African Bead Museum, on the corner of Grand River and Grand Boulevard near downtown Detroit. I parked on a block that dead-ended into a freeway, with a staid church on my right and the vibrantly patterned African Bead Museum on my left. The brick walls of the two-story building were painted in a frenzied red, yellow and black, with shards of broken mirrors interwoven into bold geometric designs. The sidewalk was filled with a multitude of unrecognizable

The entrance to Dabl's and Perette's African Bead Museum in Detroit. The chevron beads painted on the wall represent a nonverbal form of cultural transmission sorely lacking today.

scripts (at least to me), all underneath an orderly procession of juvenile maple trees. Beyond this main building lay an intriguing arrangement of artwork in an open field, a mix of painted cars, stones sitting in chairs, and piled up paint cans in some kind of fort. All of this artwork was arranged in front of what had initially caught my eye, a two-story multi-family boarded-up house decorated with vivid geometric patterns and the ubiquitous shards of mirror.

Once inside, I found Dabl presiding over a glass countertop with rows upon rows of hanging beads surrounding him on all walls. He is a large stout man, especially compared with my own skinny self, with close-cropped hair and an introspective air that gives a thoughtful and measured cadence to his deep voice. Over the next few hours I would receive not just a detailed history of the African bead, but also a multitude of ideas about how art, language and writing can either keep cultures enslaved on the path to destruction, or be used as tools of wisdom to help us integrate ourselves with the natural world. Finally, I would learn the motives behind his unsanctioned decorating of the two-story boarded-up home, and how this was an amazing example of bringing "art" (Dabl despised this word) back to its original purpose of preserving history and conveying cultural stories in an unwritten format.

Beads have a long history in all pre-European African societies, especially with the semi-nomadic pastoralists of sub-Saharan Africa, and their origin was considered mystical. Originally made of wood, bone, shells and stone, their diversity of color and meaning flourished after the introduction of glass beads from the Middle East in 200–300 AD, and became crucially important for pastoralists. These glass beads were often further enhanced by local tribes, and some parts of Africa began manufacturing their own glass beads by the Middle Ages. Beads were used to convey position and marital status and represent ancestors, but especially, along with patterned textiles, to tell the stories of the tribe. More sedentary clans in the wetter parts of Africa also used beads, but supplemented them with artifacts such as carvings, masks and other totems. All these things assisted in keeping alive the oral traditions and stories that shaped and directed these cultures. While Dabl was an expert in the bead and its role in Africa specifically, I found myself generalizing much of what he said to indigenous cultures around the world. Ultimately, he was asking me a profound question: Is art or even literature sustainable? Or does it result in patterns of thought that ultimately separate us and our culture from the natural world? According to Dabl, as an African-American he is part of a population that has been marginalized and whose history and culture have been co-opted. There was not much to disagree with there. But he then argued that forsaking an oral tradition based on handcrafted artifacts in favor of art and the written word, and later the televised image, took a form of story transmission out of the natural world and the community, and isolated it in the mind and the individual. Likewise, the idea of the lone artist working in isolation to create works of "genius" separated from tradition and any cultural story forced the audience for this art to think in terms of these objects being inaccessible and without historical meaning. Such objects are not to be touched and their interpretation is ambiguous and often incomprehensible. They are not a part of day-to-day life and their utility is dispensable.

More traditional methods of cultural transfer like beads and other physical creations, the kind of stuff we would describe as being created by artisans, have been denigrated and eradicated to great effect and, according to Dabl, replaced with stories and religions that are anthropocentric and no longer in the control of the people that need them. Although I've heard similar arguments before, it was great to hear it explained from a minority perspective and put in terms of our relationship with creative expression.

One book that had a profound effect upon me in this regard is Chellis Glendinning's *My Name is Chellis and I'm in Recovery From Western Civilization*. Chellis does a wonderful job laying out how our move from a nomadic lifestyle to agricultural domestication ten thousand years ago started a spiral of disconnection from the natural world that we had evolved with over tens of thousand of generations. This disconnection can be regarded as a massive ongoing trauma that has disrupted and almost destroyed our sense of safety and well-being on the Earth. We then react to this trauma with compulsive and addictive behavior that further disassociates us from ourselves, and leads to destructive actions that further traumatize ourselves and our descendents. Books like this have led to a field called eco-psychology that examines our disconnection from the natural world and tries to help us create a deeper understanding of our loss and the resulting compulsive behaviors, like non-stop technological addictions and trying to replace the hole in our hearts with more material goods, that seem to provide short-term fixes but exacerbate our original trauma of disconnection.

Although persuasive as all get out, arguments like these are ultimately frustrating in the vague solutions they offer and their pining away for a lost world it is no longer possible to recreate. Somehow we have to figure out a way to apply those primal connections to our current existence to restore the damage done to our individual and collective psyches and to the Earth itself. There has to be a way to cultivate an enduring compromise between our domesticated and wild selves, and to show that this is a more fulfilling life that others caught up in destructive behavior will want to emulate.

So as Dabl continued his explanation, I kept thinking to myself, what are we going to do about it? If artistic expression originally had the purpose of keeping alive the history of a culture and integrating a given people with their surrounding ecology, but has now been lost or co-opted to keep us isolated and anxiety-ridden, are we simply doomed to be blown in the wind like a decaying plastic bag? We can't go back to being pastoralists on the plains of Africa.

Seeming to understand my frustration on this issue, Dabl got up from his perch behind the counters full of ancient beads and took me on a tour of the property. His magnum opus lay sprawled out in the field behind the shop, the paint cans and chairs and stones sitting in chairs. The piece is titled *Iron Teaching Rocks How to Rust*. It involved about a dozen different staging areas and was assembled with discarded urban detritus and painted with vivid reds, yellows and greens. Dabl is working to create living artwork that transfers a cultural story of meaning and history to its viewers. This story centers around the interwoven existence of iron, stone and wood, the foundations for humanity's physical culture, and is based on his interpretation of a synthesis of African tradition. Dabl spun a long tale, not all of which I followed, to be honest, even though I've watched my video of him explaining it many times since. It involves a long saga of iron being freed from stone, iron engaging in a civil war, and stones escaping during the tumult. Other parts were more immediately comprehensible. A piece involving four timbers set out in a cross with stones on each point and in the middle represented the four stages of life. A big part of Dabl's complaint about what he considered "outside" religions (he was referring to non-animist religions like Islam and Christianity introduced into Africa) is the concept of having to be judged once you die. He argued persuasively that belief in religions that judge you when you die not only goes a long way towards creating a fear of death, but also impedes the processing and passing on of cultural

Part of *Iron Teaching Rocks How to Rust*. To the left of the car, chunks of concrete sit in chairs to learn from the tangle of metal wire before them.

knowledge during the final quarter of life. Rather than creating an expectation of becoming an ancestor who advises their progeny after death, making the accumulation of knowledge and wisdom in later life attractive, Western religions create a horrendous stress in the elderly by pushing them up against a time when they might burn in hell forever. Regardless, knowledge is obliterated when the living can no longer turn to their ancestors for advice.

Part of *Iron Teaching Rocks How to Rust* was a large iconic figure, which Dabl referred to as an *mkissi*, an iconic figure that is empowered with the help of iron. The mkissi played a central role in achieving two things. First, it kept vandals away. And secondly, it made all of the public artwork, including the heavily painted two-story abandoned building next door, invisible to the city officials. This is very important, because that building did not belong to Dabl or the African Bead Museum, and its decoration could potentially bring about two unwanted consequences. Either it could hasten the building's demolition because of its "unsightliness." Or the city could try to force the Bead Museum to take possession of the building because they are "using" it and thus charge them property tax.

Prior to its decoration and protection by the mkissi, the building was simply abandoned and had become a haven for prostitution and drug use. Dabl had continued his physical storytelling onto this abandoned home. The most conspicuous decorations were three giant blue, red and white chevron beads painted across the front on the first story. This style of glass bead was commonly made in Venice in the Middle Ages and exported to West Africa, where it became incorporated into the existing bead culture and traditional storytelling. There were also many jagged pieces of mirror worked into the design. Mirrors are important, according to Dabl, as a means of communicating with ancestors. They also reflect the sun, and the fact that it is possible to catch the fire of the sun by using correctly placed mirrors makes them an extension of the sun. There was one additional benefit of mirrors. They have the power to make potential wrongdoers become self-aware. Destructive behavior like crack cocaine use and vandalism are things people like to do in the dark where they keep their wrongdoing

Dabl telling it like it is in front of the abandoned building he helped decorate with painted chevrons and applied mirrors to assist in its preservation.

shielded from their own consciousness. But mirrors break through these shadows and bring consciousness to the surface. This is who you are and this is what you are doing, they say. There is no hiding. In the almost fifteen years since Dabl started the project, there has been no vandalism, squatting or interference from public officials. So the decorating, the storytelling and the guarding by the mkissi have been effective in preserving this building until someone can be found who wants to occupy it usefully. Rather than be a deteriorating eyesore ripe for arsonists or demolition by the city, the building relates some of Africa's history to the surrounding African-American community.

Maybe one of the most interesting things about Dabl's work was that he refused to be the only person helping to save buildings in this manner. When I asked him whether he would continue decorating any other nearby structures with the hopes of saving them, he said he wouldn't. He couldn't handle more than one. If members of the community became inspired and wanted to decorate abandoned buildings on their own, he would more than encourage it, and help to procure paint and mirrors as necessary. But he couldn't be a one-man community. Others had to get involved.

I moved on from some of the questions Dabl was raising to the first reason that Detroit had piqued my interest — its urban farming movement. It is currently illegal for gardening to be the primary use for any parcel of land in the city limits of Detroit. The city has a nationwide reputation as a innovator in using abandoned land for farming and gardening, and with 40 square miles (25,600 acres) of vacant land, you would think city leaders would be all about having more of it used for productive good rather than sitting idle. But the law hasn't changed. The good news is that, like most of the laws in Detroit, most folks just don't give a damn what it is. Usually it's too complicated to know, and whatever it is, the city's law enforcement have bigger fish to fry.

How do laws that prohibit growing your own food arise? How did we stray so far from personal independence and local reliance that a government official could tell you you can't grow food on your own land? I had some insights into these questions over the last few years back in my hometown of Durham, North Carolina. In some ways Durham is like a mini-Detroit. We thrived on the tobacco industry in the early decades of the 1900s, growing prosperous and attracting a lot of immigrants, many of them African-American, from the surrounding countryside. A thriving middle class developed with the success of this notorious product (I won't go into the debate of whether the automobile or the cigarette is more evil — that would be too long a digression). Some of the largest African-American-owned businesses in the country eventually became based in Durham, mostly on Parrish Street downtown, which became known as the Black Wall Street.

As the cigarette manufacturing base eroded in the 1970s and '80s due to reduced smoking rates and the loss of factories to lower-cost sites, especially overseas, our downtown turned into a gang-riddled wasteland. Many of the whites had fled to the burbs. Those that stayed in control of city government banned chickens and other livestock from within the city limits. Generally speaking, the upper-class whites saw banning livestock as a way of maintaining property values. The black community took it as an affront to their independence, yet another way of keeping them down. This all came to a head in the last few years when a mixed-race group of homeowners, albeit predominantly white, sought to overturn the chicken ban. Mostly people of both races didn't have any problem with overturning the old law banning chickens, but a vociferous leader of a local African-American organization raised absolute hell about it. This ornery octogenarian woman screamed bloody murder about black people being barred from having chickens for decades but now that white folks wanted them, the law was going to change. The problem was, she was mostly right. She may not have done a good job of choosing her battles, but I understood her anger.

I bring this story up for a few reasons. The first is to point out that existing laws that get in the way of allowing potentially sustainable

Just inside the gate at D-Town Farm. This spot was formerly an abandoned park that had turned into a giant dump.

activities probably have complicated social reasons for their enact-
ment. Challenging a law is generally much more complicated than
just pointing out how ridiculous it is. Although I appreciate all the
hard work the Durham group did to make chickens legal, part of me
wonders if it was worth it. What if everyone who wanted chickens just
went ahead and got them? What official would have spent the time to
do anything about it? The second point is a random observation on
what I've noticed can be a difficulty in bringing lower-income and/
or marginalized minorities into the sustainability movement. To the
extent that living a sustainable life means operating within the confines of petty bureaucratic agencies and statutes that may historically
have existed as means of segregation and constraint, it is likely to be
unappealing to sections of society that have seen the law as a force of
repression rather than as an agent of justice. It's important to consider
whether working within the existing system is of any inherent value,
and whether doing so might potentially promote or hinder progress
toward other laudable goals such as greater racial and income equality. Each case will no doubt be unique, but I think it is a question
worth asking. I hope the reader can be tolerant of my rather simplistic
thoughts on these matters. Being a Southerner, I've learned you have
to acknowledge racial issues, even if you do it clumsily, rather than
pretending they don't exist.

My urban agriculture visit took me to a few community gardens,
the biggest being D-Town Farm, run by the Detroit Black Community Food Security Network. That's a mouthful and it's almost impossible for me to remember this name without looking it up. I headed
on over to their plot of land in River Rouge Park. Driving in Detroit is
fun because even though there are No Parking signs all over the place,
there's so much empty road people don't pay any attention to them. I
followed their example and blocked an unneeded lane of traffic with
my old Saturn.

The two-acre spread was protected with seven-foot wire fenc-
ing for deer. A row of turned-out tires painted white and filled with
flowers guides visitors through the main gate. It's a lovely spot if you
stay in the garden proper, flanked as it is on three sides by dense

Jackie Hunt, vice-president of DBCFSN, with the day's harvest of melons.
One was a little too ripe and I convinced her we should eat it. Yum!

woods. Stout rows of kale and onions beckoned me onwards. I lucked
out and soon found one of the board members, vice-president Jackie
Hunt, just beginning a tour. D-Town Farm has pulled together solo
gardeners into a community farm where they can share resources like
tools and greenhouse space. At first they met reluctance from city officials about using the park for their farm. Historically, River Rouge
Park was a city park in the traditional sense, like Central Park. It was
laid out by landscape architects and was cultivated as a tame version
of wild nature where city residents could escape the noise and bustle
of the city. But then whoever was supposed to take care of it forgot to,
or got fired or just never got paid, and the whole thing turned first into
a colossal urban dump and then became so tangled with briars and
broken bottles that folks couldn't even dump shit there anymore. And
then most everyone just forgot about the entire place because it was
filled with mosquitoes and crackheads and was flat-out disgusting.

But then Malik Yakini, a local activist and owner of The Black Star Community Book Store, came in with a bunch of volunteers and cleared out their space and started planting veggies. Many of their concerns, such as high unemployment, lack of available fresh food, and abandoned lots coalesced around the idea of a vibrant local farm within the city limits. A few years on, they grow much of their members' fresh produce and have a spot at one the many farmers markets in Detroit, selling their extras and creating a few part-time jobs for hardworking youth. I enjoyed my tour and visited their booth at the farmers market later that afternoon to buy some veggies. Like many urban farms in Detroit, on one level the place is still in violation of the law even though park officials eventually gave it their blessing — its primary purpose is for farming, something that is explicitly forbidden by the city's ordinances. But there's no one to enforce it, and even if there was, who would want to tell a bunch of hardworking folks that they can't reclaim an overgrown eyesore and use it to feed their families? It's a kind of deregulation by bankruptcy and apathy — not, in my opinion, the best way to go about things, but marginally effective nonetheless. As folks who are concerned about the well-being of our earth, we want laws that maintain the privilege of business-as-usual freight-train-to-planetary-annihilation dismantled, but not at the cost of those laws that help alleviate injustice, socioeconomic inequality and clean air and water. As resources dwindle and our consumerist economy continues to falter as a consequence, funding for our municipal, state and federal governments will be under constant strain, conceivably for the remainder of our lifetimes and beyond. Transitioning to a sustainable existence will mean taking a hard look at existing regulations and trying to weed out the good from the bad, unless things get so far gone that we all end up like Detroit, having to operate under a blanket of bureaucratic regulations that, even if they're not enforced, do nothing but distract us and make us feel even more insecure.

2

Community Food

HOW CAN FOOD BE ILLEGAL? It's pretty easy to understand in our excessively property rights-oriented society how using land that isn't legally yours, like D-Town Farm and some other gardeners in Detroit, would irk the powers that be, but sitting down and eating a meal prepared by a neighbor? Twice on my travels I had the opportunity to witness the inner workings of community kitchens and watch them prepare local and organic meals that would cause the finickiest of eaters to salivate. Eating the one clandestine meal I actually got to sink my fork into, in the living room of a foreclosed home in Detroit, brought to mind being a tippler during Prohibition, the experience that much more heightened by a feeling of silly misbehavior. My father's grandparents had run a speakeasy in Prohibition Milwaukee, and I felt, just a little, that I was channeling their maverick natures.

Food is one of the most amazing ways of bringing people together. Growing food not only connects us with the earth, but like the community gardens I visited in Detroit, it connects us with our neighbors. We work beside each other, get dirty together, battle bugs and heat, and then marvel at the bounty of the earth.

But the community-building aspect of food doesn't stop there. Its most important place in this regard is sharing a meal together.

Spending time cooking and eating together is often the primary place
and time for families to be with one another, share their hopes and
frustrations, and enjoy the wonders of satisfying the most primal
of needs. Its importance is unique to the point of holiness. Think of
Christ's Last Supper, the breaking of bread after a day of fasting during
Ramadan, or a Passover Seder. By sharing meals with one another we
create bonds that are enduring and magical.

The food we don't have the time, energy or space to grow and
cook ourselves can also be an excellent opportunity for expanding
our roots in the community. Shopping at farmers markets, actually

One of Brett Bloom's DIY urban bat boxes, in the front yard of the lovely
home he set me up in.

getting to know the people who grow your food and supporting their vast efforts, buying your victuals from community-owned cooperative groceries and eating at local restaurants that patronize nearby farms help bring that community-building magic to life.

Much of this was in evidence when I stopped for a few days in a small midwestern college town on the advice of Brett Bloom, a virtual acquaintance who has spearheaded an amazing variety of grassroots projects. Among a dozen other goings-on, Brett and his wife were moving to Denmark just before I arrived. How he had the time to correspond with a meandering writer and give me not just platterfuls of mind-bogglingly cool leads all across the country, but also set me up with a place to stay and home-cooked meals from the director of the farmers market, Lisa BK and her husband Jim, I'll never understand. In the front yard garden of the quaint bungalow where he arranged for me to stay was a testament to his last project, a bat box on a 12-foot pole. Bringing nature into urban environments through DIY community-led projects is one of Brett's modus operandi, more of which can be found at temporaryservices.org, and I know that small college town is worse off for their departure.

Unfortunately, the first news I received in this idyllic burg, trapped though it is on all sides by a never-ending industrial corn desert, was grim. The self-described "underground chocolatier" that I had been intent on meeting had died the day before. We had traded a few e-mails and already set up a lunch date for me to hear his story. This depressing news sucked the wind from my sails and my first inclination was to lock myself up in the house and recover for a few days from the intense heat wave that had just broke.

But the little college town, and especially farmers market director Lisa BK, had too much pulsating energy to allow me to sit still for long. Much of what was on offer in the form of the local food movement was aboveboard, as should be expected. The thriving farmers market and a newly expanded cooperative grocery were testament to the community's love of food, all the more poignant for it being not just stuck in the midst of vast fields of genetically modified corn, but also home to the state's Ag university, a sprawling complex of labs and experimental fields where probably only the devil himself knows what heinous crimes were being perpetrated against mother nature.

The co-op was very interesting to me, mostly because I was on the board of a start-up cooperative grocery, Durham Central Market, back home. I interviewed Jacqueline, the general manager, getting great advice on fundraising ideas, but then as we starting talking about my book project, an interesting little gem popped out. Jacqueline told me about a clandestine community-supported kitchen run out of their home by a local couple, Ben and Kate, who did a lot of their shopping at the co-op. With a quick phone introduction from Jacqueline, I was in.

I jumped on my borrowed bike and pedaled over to their home, just a few blocks from where I was staying. Ben and Kate were at home waiting on a delivery from a local farm. As we chatted about their enterprise for an hour or so, I was struck by how thoroughly sincere and respectable this couple was. They were both obviously motivated by a deep passion for food and their neighbors, and imbued with a stellar work ethic. Their two young boys frolicked on the patterned rug in their cozy living room as we spoke. Bonnie and Clyde they were not. Here were wholesome outlaws making delicious food for their community, in contrast to the legalized crimes being perpetrated by many of the farms just outside of town, whose excess fertilizers and pesticides flow down the Mississippi to poison the Gulf of Mexico, and whose third-rate product is force fed to sick cows in concentrated feed lots a few states to the west, making vast swaths of our country reek of shit and death.

So how did the idea of a community-supported kitchen come about? And what makes it illegal? In many municipalities, exchanging prepared food for money is illegal, unless it comes from an inspected kitchen such as a restaurant or catering business, or is done at the client's home by a personal chef. But Ben and Kate had come across a demand for something in the middle that was neither a restaurant, catering or being a personal chef, and they did so quite by accident. A friend who had done some underground catering gave Ben a call, to see if he would be interested in preparing two to four meals a week for

Ben and Kate's little boy does a little quality control with the shiitakes before they go on the stove.

an acquaintance named Nancy, something the friend himself wasn't interested in. The idea of being a personal chef didn't appeal to Ben, but he and Kate sat down one Sunday at a cafe and gave the idea a thorough going over. While preparing meals for one family would require a huge expense to make it feasible, it didn't take long to figure out that it wouldn't add that many more hours of work to radically increase the number of meals prepared, and hence the potential number of customers. The idea of community-supported agriculture, where shares of veggies grown on a farm are allotted to customers and are paid for in advance, quickly sprung to mind. Why not do the same thing with prepared meals? Customers could pay in advance and then receive a few dinners a week, all prepared from fresh, local ingredients. Ben was getting burned out as a manager on a local farm, and had plenty of chef experience. Working at home would allow both he and Kate to work together and take care of their expanding family. The idea of the community-supported kitchen was born.

Ben and Kate told Nancy about their willingness to cook for her, but only if she could help round up a few more customers to see if the model would work. In early October of 2007, they had the customers and were ready to try it out. They made stir-fried vegetables with garlic sauce and sweet potato noodles for one meal, and a second of eggplant dumplings with roasted red pepper sauce and couscous. They were a hit. More shares came in, a few more each month, and the business started to take off. Starting a business is never easy, and Ben and Kate had their work cut out for them. Kate was working full time during the day, Ben was waiting tables three or four nights a week, and their nine-month-old boy needed constant attention. Being a local food outlaw was no walk in the park.

But the strain of preparing more and more meals (they had a target of 50 customers) in a cramped kitchen with seven-foot ceilings, a leaky roof, no exhaust, little room for racks to put food coming out of the oven, crappy lighting and old appliances quickly made the project seem untenable in the existing circumstances. It was crunch time. Do they look to rent a place, outfit it with all the required but not always

Edamame and red peppers on noodles, one of the delicious meals coming out of Ben and Kate's community-supported kitchen.

Credit: Kate L.

Kate in the revamped kitchen that allowed their community-supported
kitchen to expand to fifty customers.

necessary equipment to become health code compliant, or do they
risk a remodel of their existing kitchen — against zoning regulations
that prohibit mixed commercial and residential uses — for a third of
the cost so they can continue to take care of their boy, with another
infant on the way, and greatly increase the value of their home? The
latter, of course, was against the law, but other than that, all logic
pointed towards it. Their customers did not care if their food was
coming out of an inspected kitchen. They knew Ben and Kate personally and trusted them implicitly to not only prepare their food using
as many local and organic ingredients as possible, but to also keep
their kitchen clean. There were other financial and ecological costs
to consider as well between the two options. An inspected kitchen
likely meant using one-time disposable containers for delivery, and
having to "sanitize" all their kitchen equipment using chlorine bleach.
Harmful bacteria levels are pretty much equivalent whether kitchen

equipment is washed using bleach, a vinegar/water solution, or hot, soapy water. Yet health code regulations require bleach. Chlorine is a toxic substance, proven to cause bladder, rectal and breast cancers. Vinegar is not toxic — it is food. When you personally know the customers you are cooking for, these decisions make a big difference.

Beyond being more in tune with their ethics and long-term financial well-being (because it was cheaper and improved the value of their home), it turns out the decision to stay underground meant success rather than financial ruin for Ben and Kate in the short term too. A month into the kitchen remodel in late summer 2008, the economy went into a nosedive. America's obsession with flimsy housing built in sprawled-out suburbs and its addiction to easy credit and cheap oil had finally collided with reality, bringing our country to the precipice of financial collapse. The stock market bit the dust and foreclosures went through the roof. Subscriptions to Ben and Kate's community-supported kitchen fell in half. Their hearts skipped beats whenever a new customer would cancel or, increasingly rarely, sign up. If they had been saddled with a $100,000 loan and rent on a separate space, bankruptcy would have been all but assured. They sat tight, concentrating on the quality of their meals, finishing the revamped kitchen, strengthening ties to local farms and trying not to freak out. It worked. By the next fall subscriptions started to pick up again, and by the spring of 2010 they had achieved their goal of 50 customers. The business was a success.

Here was an enterprise that was bringing healthy, fresh, delicious, local food to customers who needed the extra time to take kids to music lessons, stay late at work or just have some free time puttering around. It supported local farms and provided meaningful work to a couple who loved food, and allowed them to take care of their children at home. Yet it was impossible to accomplish this within the existing structure of the county's health codes and zoning laws. Their community-supported kitchen was an untested model, and starting an untested business doesn't make sense if you have to plunk down 100 G's before you can see if it works. Ben and Kate would love for their business to be legit, not least of all so that they can show others that it's a working, replicable model. But supporting a compliant kitchen away from home would require substantially more than fifty customers. First of all, it wasn't clear how many additional customers there would be in their small town, but it would also require additional employees, and Ben and Kate had no desire to manage anyone.

So here is an example of regulation, originally required to ensure that larger food businesses do not sell unsafe products, ending up prohibiting the formation of smaller food businesses. To sum up the history: food businesses got too large and started making people sick. Governments required inspections and health codes. Political influence by these large businesses then tweaked the health laws to prevent smaller competitors from entering the market. Less competition made for bigger food companies, resulting in more food poisoning and necessitating even more regulation.

This all played out according to script with the Food Safety Modernization Act of late 2010. Massive agribusiness concerns mix different types of food inputs from all over the country, using waste from concentrated feed lots and slaughterhouses for growing fruits and vegetables. On a small scale and with proper composting, livestock waste is beneficial to farming, and the limited distances food from smaller farms travels makes spreading diseases and pathogens unlikely. But just like everything else in life, what is good in small doses quickly becomes poisonous in larger ones. Industrial farming's callous production techniques and enormous waste creation, combined with the relentless transportation of inputs around the country, has led in recent years to contamination of a wide variety of once "safe" crops such as strawberries and spinach with potentially life-threatening pathogens like e. coli and salmonella. The events of the past decade played out in the media, and some kind of political action finally became unavoidable. Tracking food from Big Agriculture became necessary, because of its nationwide and even international distribution. Being able to trace food to its source on such a large scale requires tracking equipment such as bar codes and computer recording equipment, and more frequent (or, I should say, less infrequent) inspections. There are a lot of fixed costs involved in this, and as with all fixed costs, the larger the operation, the easier it is to spread out those costs. The original intent of the law was to apply it to *all* farms, no matter their size, even though tracking food that is only sold in nearby markets and groceries is much easier, to say nothing of the fact that local food is much less likely to be contaminated. Big Ag was initially in favor of the law, because they knew it would pretty much wipe out their smaller competition, and at least give the appearance of a safer food distribution system. Most small farms would not be able to cope with the increased costs, and Big Ag knew it. Fortunately, agitation from those concerned with the health of their local food networks resulted in the Tester-Hagan amendment. Although far from perfect, it does exempt many smaller farms (less than $500,000 in revenue) from the law's provisions. Big Ag did an immediate about-face once the amendment was introduced and tried to kill the law, but it went through anyway. Without the vigilance of local food activists, most small farms nationwide would have been driven underground.

Of course Big Ag screamed unfair. What's fair about a marketplace that applies different rules to different entities, based solely on their size? It's interesting to consider the alternative: a regulation-free environment where "the invisible hand," so supposedly beloved by big business types, was allowed to operate. In this scenario, Big Ag would of course continue its race to the bottom. It would use the cheapest inputs possible, treat workers as callously as possible and try to make up for poor quality with expensive advertising and marketing. Since large outbreaks of disease have happened frequently even with some regulation, the likely result would be even more contamination. With such a complex chain of operations, it would be impossible to pinpoint where these large outbreaks of disease might have originated. The reputation of cheap food from Big Ag would be under constant bombardment. You would literally be risking the lives of yourself and your family every time you ate their food.

Unlike with such large-scale operations, Ben and Kate's community-supported kitchen, like small-scale food producers everywhere, is directly responsible to their consumers. To quote Ben: "As a business grows, quality declines. In food at least, this relationship between size and quality is absolute and immediate. Given that this relationship exists, scale-appropriate regulation acknowledges the relationship between growth and responsibility. A business should not be rewarded for unlimited growth without oversight, nor should it be penalized for investing in quality preservation and artisanal scale."

An outbreak of sickness among Ben and Kate's customers would likely be catastrophic for their business. In addition, they know and *care* about the people they are serving. They are their neighbors. Their kids play together. They live in the same neighborhood. They run into each other at the co-op. Direct human-to-human interactions between producer and consumer are *the* most effective form of regulation there can ever be.

I know nothing about running any kind of professional kitchen. I love to garden and cook, so I understand seasonality, but my meals are always cooked slowly, in small volumes, generally done with a cold beer or glass of wine in hand, and served immediately. My only restaurant experience was working at a Pizza Hut for two months when I was eighteen. I was unable to eat pizza for years afterwards. Talking with Ben made the stories I'd heard from friends who worked at or owned restaurants hit home. It takes a tremendous amount of work to get delicious local food to waiting customers.

The foundation of Ben and Kate's community-supported kitchen is the local farms where they get the lion's share of their vegetables, dairy and meat. Deep midwestern soils, ample rainfall and plenty of summer sun ensures foods of the highest quality can be grown. Of course, these amazing inputs are mostly used to grow cheap #2 corn by the silo-full, much of it used to feed our starving automobiles or make cows sick before they're slaughtered. But fortunately the surrounding land, the farmers market and the co-op in their little burg support a great variety of dedicated farmers growing yummy veggies, raising pasture-raised pork, beef and chicken, and crafting artisanal cheeses. Deepening the relationship between their kitchen and the local farms is predicated on a respectful relationship, primarily with three local farms, one of which Ben used to manage. The farms know they are committed to buying their products, they give the farms as much lead time as possible for orders, there's no haggling or cross-competing, and they often purchase surpluses at a somewhat reduced price. Their buying consistently and buying big makes the relationship worthwhile to the farms.

Running the kitchen requires skill in cooking seasonally, and most importantly, planning ahead. The summer months are grueling. This is when huge quantities of produce are prepped and either frozen or canned, at some considerable risk to the enterprise, since memberships are monthly and Ben and Kate are putting away food for the winter. Hundreds of pounds of tomatoes are canned, fresh corn is frozen, pestos and other sauces are prepared in bulk and frozen for the long, cold winters. The true test of a community-supported kitchen, in Mark's words, are "managing and planning for using local foods year-round artfully and gracefully."

Ben pulling a ham cut from a locally-raised Tamsworth pig out of its salt bath, on its way to being prosciutto.

Credit: Kate L.

You have to be a big-time foodie to make one of these things work. The hours are long. Delivering the two meals for each member on Tuesday afternoons entails six days of prep and planning. Thursday the menu is planned and all the produce and meats are ordered. On Friday, they're delivered and stored in preparation for cooking. Saturday is for shopping at the farmers market and the co-op for smaller items. Sunday often means soaking beans and other minor prep work like pulling goods from the freezer to thaw. Monday is the big prep day, and Ben and Kate tag-team taking care of the kids with working in the kitchen. Fillings, sauces and bread doughs are made. Some items, like soups, are packaged up Monday evening. But by the end of the day the kitchen has to be clean and ready to go for the big day.

Tuesday is when it all comes together. Ben is up and cooking by 7 AM. Breads go in the oven, and then the most technically difficult foods are assembled. More subtly flavored foods like salads and rice dishes are saved for last to keep them as fresh as possible, as are garnishes and dressings. Packing everything up has to start by noon, and it's no mean task. Ben takes care of the kids and Kate takes over in the kitchen, breaking down portions according to how many shares there are by household. There are distinct containers (mostly glass) for separate portions of the meal as well as for portion size. Their proper number has to be calculated, retrieved from storage and wiped clean. The meals are portioned out by weight, then lidded or cellophaned. The final part of assembly is packing the entire meal into a reusable, color-coded grocery bag, with the containers on the bottom and more delicate items like bags of salad on top. Different colored bags are for specific diets — vegetarian, gluten-free, etc. Next the bags go into coolers and the coolers are loaded into the station wagon. All this needs to be done by 2 PM. The 24 separate deliveries take about two hours. Finally, it's all done and Ben and Kate get to enjoy dinner with their kids, knowing they have Wednesday to themselves.

Unfortunately, I didn't get to taste one of Ben and Kate's scrumptious meals. My timing was wrong, having shown up on a weekend when only minor prep work was happening. This bummed me out, so I was all the more excited when I stumbled upon another clandestine kitchen in Detroit on the tail end of my trip. While I was on my tour of the D-Town farm, I watched as another member of the tour pulled out a bag and began stuffing it with purslane, a troublesome weed that volunteers spent many hours yanking out of the garden beds. I have a funny relationship with this plant. It has always piqued my curiosity, being one of the more choice edible weeds, high in Omega-3s and a great soup thickener. But for the life of me, I've never been able to get it to grow. I'd hypothesized that it's because of the long hot summers in North Carolina, but a summer or two back I was walking along the highway in Birmingham, Alabama, (don't ask) and found a patch of purslane sprouting out of the scalding black pavement, semis rumbling by, as happy as could be. Some weeds, I guess, are just stubborn, and value their independence above all else. They won't be civilized in a garden patch.

I couldn't help but inquire about the purslane's ultimate destination. The woman, Rakiza, explained she was going to chop it up and put it in a salad for a dinner club she was having later that evening. After some more conversation, and, I expect, some sizing me up on her part, she extended an invitation. She apologized for having to charge for the meal. Little did she know that this would only pique my interest that much more. After some additional inquiry, I learned she was running a raw/vegan speakeasy restaurant every Thursday out of the foreclosed home she was housesitting for a friend. I won't pretend that I eat raw or vegan very often, but after five weeks on the road eating peanut butter sandwiches and greasy diner eggs, I could feel my colon jumping for joy at the thought.

I showed up that evening, and found a cast of characters from the African-American community of Detroit not often represented in the media. About a dozen folks cycled through over the course of a few hours, many nattily dressed, all devoted to their health and the well-being of their beloved city. There were a fair number of single men, and I can sympathize with the difficulty of cooking healthy meals when alone at home. Teachers, salesmen and delivery drivers came in, served themselves up a plate of raw zucchini-noodle lasagna with a blendered squash-seed filling, a delicious salad with the aforementioned purslane and many other greens, peeled carrots and slices of red peppers, and all washed down with fresh lemonade and apple cider.

There was much talk of the city's troubles and the poor health of Detroit's citizenry and how that has likely led to much of its social decline. I couldn't help but butt in and offer some words of encouragement. Okay, Detroit had fallen on hard times, there was no denying that, but I had to give my kudos to everyone in the room, who by concerning themselves with their own health and well-being were acting to reinvigorate their city at its core. Just like the subscribers to Ben and Kate's community-supported kitchen, the folks spending ten dollars for a scrumptious meal once a week in that quaint foreclosed home were helping to employ Rakiza and her cooking partner, as well as providing revenue for local farms. They were literally sowing the seeds for their community's revival amongst its decay.

An Interview with Ben

I began by asking Ben what membership in his community-supported kitchen means.

Membership is the keystone of our business.

Membership is what differentiates our business model from that of the personal chef, caterer or a restaurant. Underlying the membership premise is the concept of commitment and relationships.

First of all, members pay us in advance, not a la carte. This financial commitment helps us manage our cash flow and make purchasing decisions with minimized risk, thus allowing us to control our overhead. This in turn allows us to keep membership dues affordable. This concept is radically different from the restaurant model in which owners accept considerable risk buying food in anticipation of sales that may or may not be realized. High mark-ups, decreased quality, and waste become accepted practices.

Secondly, members commit to taking their shares every week of the month. Of course, we are flexible with travel plans or unforeseen circumstances. But in general, if you are here, you agree to receive your share. Again, this helps us know what our monthly income will be and allows us to make business and personal decisions accordingly. Mitigating our risk and providing financial stability, so different from waiting tables or event catering, again reciprocates in keeping prices affordable for the members. We have yet to raise prices, and have even offered discounts for members who commit to every week for the academic calendar (September to June). If they need to miss a week or so, they still pay for the whole month, but we allocate their missed shares into extra portions when they want them for extra-busy weeks, or when guests come to town. We happily exchange discount for stability.

For us, we are committed to constancy. Having members means that we are committed to providing meals for them *every* week. When the weather is snowy, we do our damnedest to deliver. When it is sweltering, we still fire up the stove. When one of us falls ill, the other picks up the slack and friends and family come to the rescue with child care. We time our travels with the majority of our members', and we never, never just flake out ("Hey everybody! Just a quick e-mail to let you know that we decided to stay an extra night in Madison to catch a Willy Nelson show, so deliveries will be on Wednesday! Thanks for understanding!!!"). Never. We need our members and, I dare say, they need us.

We are committed to professionalism. We do our best and push our skills to deliver excellent quality meals each week and to accommodate special dietary needs. Learning about gluten-free baking recently is a great example. It also means that we are committed to our slogan of local, seasonal and organic and our mantra of "Quality pays." We don't have an explicit contract, but I know our members assume that we are using the best quality local and organic food that we can. When the pressure of food costs squeezes us, and I am faced with choosing local/organic over conventional, I know what my members are expecting me to do. I do use some conventional produce, but as a last choice, and often I just change the menu to fit what I *do* have as opposed to compromising to get what I want. Ultimately, membership means that we enter into a mutualistic relationship. A series of mutualistic relationships, really, because the relationships we maintain with our farmers are directly related to our membership relationships and vice versa. This differs greatly from the service, or even subservience, context of restaurant or catering work where everyone is trying to squeeze the other person for all they can get. Our model is based on trust.

For us, the CSK has been revelatory. We are finally putting together all of our seemingly disparate skills: agriculture, culinary arts, environmental education, management and urban homesteading into one cohesive piece — our business. We value having a home-based business, employment that matches our values, and an income that, while modest, allows us to grow our savings while also having a flexible, quality of life-based schedule.

To our members we offer, in exchange, an opportunity for them to also realize their own quality of life goals. The extra breathing room we give them each week helps them more readily balance their careers, their growing families, their kids' extra-curriculars and community involvement. Our members are active, involved people with strong career paths. They are educated and aware of social and environmental issues. They value the provenance and health value of our food. I imagine that many of our members make sacrifices for their careers. Eating food of inferior quality, buying into a corrupt food system or paying a premium for crap don't need to be among them.

Ultimately, we care about our members. Our work has paralleled our members through births, deaths, comings of age, sabbaticals and returns, growth and recession. I know their jobs, their homes, their families, their likes, dislikes, aversions and allergies. I can infer their income, style and politics and they, mine. We come to know each other. Feeding people in this way has a strong aspect of intimacy. It is honest work, and it enriches us.

3

Intentional Communities

THE OLD ADAGE about women (or men) could just as easily apply to people in general — you can't live with them, and you can't live without them. Human relationships would be challenging in the best of times, I imagine. Like everyone else, though, I wouldn't know. Now entering my late thirties, my life has been filled with wars against other nations, relentless technological change, and of course the never-ending destruction of the planet we live on to satisfy illusionary physical "needs" and an ever-expanding human population. In an age of trauma, disassociation from the natural world, perpetual adolescence and the threat of civilizational collapse, getting along with one another is that much more of a challenge.

But I can tell you something, at least about myself. Living alone out in the woods, even as a couple, in a house you built by yourself that is largely off the grid, is pretty boring. Unless you have an exceptionally introverted personality and get most of your satisfying relationships from nature and not human contact, such a life will ultimately ring hollow. Thoreau only spent two years in the woods.

Like everyone, I was thrown for a loop by the attacks of September 11th. My former wife and I were building our cob home out in the sticks, already interested in and applying ecological concepts like natural building and solar energy. We had friends and family in New York City whom we couldn't contact for days. The physical reality of a globalized, interconnected world was no longer something that could be ignored. Things were happening that made our lives no longer seem safe, even in our remote wooded enclave.

For me personally, this resulted in an in-depth look at the reason that the alleged perpetrator had given for attacking our nation. I use the word "alleged" purposefully, simply because no proof was ever given to prove Osama bin Laden's guilt, and because the official story of what happened on that day has more holes in it than my colander. What actually happened on that day a peon like me will never get to know, but I won't be force-fed a bunch of patriotic malarkey just to have an answer. It will remain a mystery, as it should for everyone, especially for those who are so sure of what happened one way or the other.

But if I did accept the premise that American troops in Saudi Arabia were the motivation for the attack, then I couldn't help but wonder, why did we have troops there? To say it's all about oil is to miss many of the other underpinnings of empire, but at least for Saudi Arabia, it is all about the oil. It didn't take long for me to come across a very interesting book by Kenneth Deffeyes titled *Hubbert's Peak: The Impending World Oil Shortage*. My crash course in peak oil had begun. Over the next two years, our responding to the attack by invading the last oil-rich nation in the world for exceedingly flimsy reasons fueled what I will admit was an unhealthy obsession with the topic. But here was a game-changer to a young man in his mid-twenties. Things were not just unsustainable in the long run, they looked to be so in the short run as well.

I started a discussion group that met once a month to talk about the impacts of peak oil. This had the unfortunate effect of me being seriously introduced to the topic of global climate disruption by a knowledgeable attendee. As if I didn't have problems enough already, now I had to swallow this other massive bummer of a pill. At first, our group did everything we could to raise awareness of these two topics, especially peak oil. We had only modest success, and at the time this surprised me. How could people just ignore these two world-changing topics? Didn't they want to know the truth? Frankly, no, they didn't. They were having enough trouble getting along in their personal lives without fretting about the end of civilization as they knew it. Fair enough, I suppose. If I had been able to ignore these topics and continue to live my life as it was, I probably would have been happier, at least for a few more years. Happiness is a worthy goal, for sure, but it is as ephemeral as a rainbow. And by living in a false world, I would have been sacrificing any hope for the much more vital ingredient of meaning in my life. It was just not in me to do this.

As the group grew, a few began considering radically altering their existing lives to better prepare themselves for the potential upheaval of a consumerist world torn loose from its moorings. This was in 2005. Katrina would soon devastate New Orleans, causing massive disruptions to North Carolina's fuel supplies as a result. The notion of being centered in a community capable of perpetuating itself in a relocalizing world was the main concern of this smaller group. My former wife Rebekah and I were part of this group considering a move, but our dissatisfaction with where we lived was as much centered on a general lack of available community as it was on moving to a place that would be potentially self-sufficient in a short period of time. Although a quick collapse seemed like a possibility (and still does), the idea of planning one's life around this idea is both counterproductive and impossible. It is to make a life decision based on fear, and once you start doing that, you are doomed to be either alone and starving in the woods or controlled by some outside force. Fear is the foundation of dependency. Where optimism does not exist, it must be manufactured, or there will be no hope for success.

Two members of this group were Tim Bennett and Sally Erickson, the director and producer respectively of the all-encompassing documentary *What a Way To Go: Life at the End of Empire*. Talking with both of them, along with reading the recently published 30-year update to *The Limits to Growth*, allowed me to understand some of the interconnectedness of all of the world's ecological problems. Ultimately, peak oil was one of many examples of unsustainable resource use, and global climate disruption was one of many examples of unsustainable pollution. Although both of these problems seemed to have their roots in fossil fuel use, when seen as part of an even larger problem of a fundamentally askew relationship between humans and the planet, just eliminating fossil fuel use wasn't going to resolve this disconnection. There was something deeper that needed repairing, and it centered around our relationships with each other and the natural world. Trying to figure out where and how to attempt to rebalance this relationship resulted in many long and heartfelt discussions.

Tim and Sally already lived in what to many of us seemed like the perfect little community for surviving a potentially tumultuous transition, so their interest in moving was intriguing. Blue Heron Farms was a few miles outside the small progressive burg of Pittsboro, North Carolina (more on this in Chapter 9) and was comprised of an eclectic mix of individuals who were living in and/or building thoughtful alternative homes around a mix of open fields and woods. As Rebekah and I pondered a move away from our isolation, we were fortunate to have this interesting example to provoke our thoughts. How many people would it take to build a sustainable town? Was building a town from scratch even something I thought was a good idea? It seemed obvious that Blue Heron had a long way to go in adding community members (above its two dozen or so) if it ever hoped to achieve some notion of independence.

Not that it necessarily did. Not all the other residents of Blue Heron were thinking they had to confront an imminent withering of industrial convenience. After their documentary came out, Tim and Sally eventually became frustrated with what they perceived as a too-slow response to the world's dire circumstances, and left the community. But Blue Heron remains a beautiful place with many seemingly satisfied residents. Where is the right place to live? And who do you want to live with?

Many of our lives suffer from a lack of community, so it's not surprising that there should be a movement for *intentional* communities. If community is not arising of its own accord in our modern lives, then let's make it happen. Community, of course, can happen wherever there are people. You don't have to move to a new place to increase your connections with other people, but some sort of intention and will to do so is required. To me, the most interesting idea for an intentional community is the concept of the ecovillage. The idea, basically, is to create from scratch something that approximates the self-sufficiency of a small village before industrial civilization made faraway goods readily available, and to do so with as deep and integrated a relationship with the natural world as possible. While it may be possible to develop stronger human community wherever other people are present, strengthening the wider human-nature community is perhaps less difficult in a more natural setting. Or perhaps not. My own urban experience of helping to rebuild nature in a compromised environment has certainly deepened my own connection to the surrounding ecology. Yet the concept of developing and strengthening that relationship from the get-go in an ecovillage, rather than trying to attempt something retroactively, creates a wonderful experiment in attempting to draw the boundaries between our personal needs and the needs of a thriving ecology.

Sanctuary makes a point of building higher density housing like this straw-bale "condo" to create more of a village feel.

Credit: Albert Bates

One member of our group, Martha, decided to pull up stakes with her husband and move to a well-established ecovillage tucked away in a beautiful valley up in the mountains of North Carolina, a place I'll refer to as Sanctuary, established in 1994 with the purchase of a few hundred acres and an idyllic vision of a strong community integrated with its surrounding ecology. The comprehensive nature of Sanctuary's re-evaluation of our everyday lives is what has impressed me the most in my visits over the last half decade. Yet despite their fundamentally antagonistic stance towards the status quo, they have managed to maintain a working relationship with local inspectors that has allowed for steady growth of the project. With my own experience of building a not-so-legal single residence, the concept of building an entire village that exists in a kind of hazy legal fog is intimidating and, to some extent, staggering in its confrontational potential. Effectively, the inspectors have agreed to come with blinders on, focusing only on a particular building and whether it meets their standards. Some homes get inspected, others don't. The ones that aren't treated as residences are, with a wink, regarded as "sheds" or "agricultural

A home built of cob at Sanctuary, typical of the construction techniques that focus on owner-built homes and indigenous materials.

Credit: Albert Bates

buildings." An intense dichotomy has resulted among members of the community, one of several that seems always on the verge of tearing the experiment apart. Is it better to try to work within the limits of the established law and perhaps try to change it if it's deemed too restrictive? Or better to build the way you think is right and see what, if anything, results from this more confrontational stance. The mountains are renowned for their live-and-let-live attitude, yet a change of the guard down at the permit office could still result in some tight ass with a bone to pick.

Everything about Sanctuary is experimental — its methods of building, its political organization, its interaction with the public as an educational center, its water, sewer and energy systems. This is striking, because ultimately what they want to achieve is something much less in flux. Permaculture offers the promise of a steady-state system of human and ecological interaction that rewards permanence and long-term care with accumulated wealth. Not money wealth, but rather the real wealth of well-built buildings that last centuries, rich soil from recycled nutrients, renewable energy, rainwater collection and a mature social and political organization that encourages self-development along with an interwoven community. Yet the ingredients, especially the knowledge and the people, are born of the impermanent and damaged nature of Western civilization, as we all are. Walking down the main avenue of Sanctuary, it still takes a large dose of vision to imagine a stable, functioning, sustainable society. Sixteen years of existence seems like a long time, but put in the context of what they are attempting to achieve, it still feels like day one.

It is a truly unique experience, wandering through town, though it is not such an easy thing to do. Visits are generally restricted to a few Saturdays a month, and unfamiliar faces are given scrutiny even when accompanied by salutations. It's hard not to feel at least a little like an interloper, and this highlights one of the other dichotomies that exists here: the desire to educate the public against the desire to live out from under the microscope. In a way, it's not different than you might feel wandering through a small village anywhere in the world. It's impossible to be anonymous in a small town. My visits have always had a purpose, either visiting acquaintances or buying plants from the small nursery that specializes in edible and medicinal plants.

Much of the uniqueness that Sanctuary exhibits is in the accumulation of alternative infrastructure over the years. While I've seen my fair share of alternatively built homes, they generally exist as solitary creatures, or at best in a clump of two or three in the woods. But here cob and straw bale homes, some multi-story, line the hillsides as the road curves up the small valley. Public buildings such as the meeting hall and store are similarly constructed. Passive solar is the norm, and green roofs in various states of completion add a tumbling organic nature to the many buildings that would make Frank Lloyd Wright smile. Rainwater collection tanks, some up to 10,000 gallons or more, are common besides buildings, and little humanure shacks are interspersed throughout town. A large stream provides micro-hydro juice throughout the year, shared among the residents, and PV panels are common accoutrements, although, like everywhere trees grow, how much solar access to have and how many trees to leave standing is a constant source of disagreement. Many homes seem to be in a state of perpetual construction. I've experienced this phenomenon myself. Once it gets to where you can live in it, you're so exhausted you just move in, and the details often get postponed indefinitely. While there's definitely the feeling of a town as you walk the paths and roads, there's also the feeling of haphazard incompletion. There's so much to do to build a sustainable life from scratch, and the garden and paying job often get more attention than adding trim to corners of your house.

Residents go about their daily business. There are cars here, all parked near the entrance, but none are used for getting around town, only for making forays to the grocery store, or, often, for the forty-five minute commute to Asheville for a job. There's a smattering of employment options within Sanctuary, including helping to build the infrastructure for new residents, working on the vegetable farm and the aforementioned nursery. Internet access allows a few entrepreneurs to run boutique businesses over the web. The folks you see in town, strolling, pushing a wheelbarrow of compost or lugging a post

A crowd relaxes during a conference focusing on ecological living outside the conference center at Sanctuary.

towards a construction site, are more average looking than you might expect. They're not dressed in bear skins, although many clothes are hand-sewn, and dreadlocks and beards are common.

How do all these people get along? That's what I wanted to know. If you have the opportunity to remain outside an established political system for the most part but you're more than a handful of people, what kind of laws and regulations do you come up with? Even if you're not sharing property and building all kinds of experimental structures and systems, getting sixty people together for any length of time and not having a few interpersonal clashes is impossible. I can remember some big fat juicy squabbles between my ex-wife and myself as we built our cob home, and that's only two people! How to regulate these disagreements in an equitable and sustainable fashion? At Sanctuary the opportunity exists to try and determine potential legal systems that might be key to any town being sustainable in the future.

Before describing these systems in detail, it helps to explain a few of the singular conditions that exist there that make Sanctuary unlike a typical village. First it must be mentioned that potential residents apply to become members in a lengthy process that involves several interviews and, often, a short-term stay to determine compatibility. This screening process would keep out, as you might imagine, a Rush Limbaugh-listening, giant-pickup-truck-driving redneck who thought pooping in a bucket was a heinous crime against God and country — assuming such an individual might want to live there. But it also might exclude more seemingly compatible types if they appear difficult to weave into the existing philosophy and code of ethics at Sanctuary. Because of this preselection, getting along is more akin to tempering disputes among friends than among the random set of individuals who might naturally arise in any other given village. Another factor is the high turnover of individuals at Sanctuary. Despite its attempts to be a village, Sanctuary is still part of our highly mobilized, deracinated modern world. Residents' ability to come and go relatively easily, compared to, say, villagers before the industrial revolution, has two primary effects. First, it makes forming long-lasting, trusting relationships more difficult. And secondly, it bleeds efficacy from the principal means the larger group has of enforcing socially acceptable behavior onto the individual, that is, the threat of ostracism. In a tightly knit community, the threat of temporarily severing an offender's ties to the community by social ostracism through withholding certain rights and privileges, or by physical ostracism through outright banishment, has often been used historically from hunter-gatherer societies to more settled ones.

The dwindling of the efficacy of ostracism as an enforcement mechanism is a universal problem in modern times. We have become highly mobilized and interconnected, and as a result the world has become more homogenized. Both of these things have led to a loss of a sense of place. It's no wonder that as the tool of ostracism has become less effective, the concept of the prison has come to take over its role for a greater number of offenses. If withholding social connections and privileges or banishment is insufficient punishment because your integration with your surrounding community is weak, then the next logical step is to lock you in a box if you misbehave, in effect a stay-where-you-are ostracism. This is not to justify the concept of the prison, but only to try and understand why it came about, and to understand the difficulties in creating a sufficient enforcement mechanism in a modern village. Obviously, the use of prisons has steadily expanded since their conception, especially to keep what is perceived as the underclass at bay, and now to protect all those fabulous McMansions and shiny cars that so many of us have substituted for our soul. Property is nine-tenths of the law, leaving, by my math, one-tenth for things like social welfare, community interactions and physical and ecological health. How much better off we would be if that ratio were reversed!

Don't worry. There are no prisons at Sanctuary. I've showed my hand here, in that I obviously think some kind of enforcement mechanism is required to make sure people get along. Some form of social or physical ostracism would seem to be a necessary ingredient for enforcing agreed upon rules, and the more tightly knit the community, the more effective it would be. In the longer term, Sanctuary's role as a unique place where people are thoroughly integrated into their community should make this tool more effective than it is elsewhere, but modern man's predilection for jumping ship when the times get tough currently makes creating a viable enforcement structure that is not dependent on incarceration very difficult.

With all that said, how do things such as rule enforcement and political expression work at Sanctuary? From its inception, the founders considered consensus to be a fundamental tool of a functioning village in the long term. I've pondered this amazing dedication over the last five years of my visits and found their commitment to it to border on sainthood. How on earth can you get 60 people to agree on anything? My involvement is too cursory to answer that question. I haven't sat in on any meetings and delved into the nitty-gritty of how it all works. I do know from talking to various current and former residents that the commitment to consensus is one of those big disagreements that hangs over the village. There is definitely no consensus

on consensus. Perhaps only a third of the residents actively participate in most decisions, unless the topic is one that really fires folks
up. But the thought of getting even 20 people to agree on something
sounds next to impossible. Yet over the last 16 years they have slogged
through and managed to pull it off. To my mind, it's one thing to try
to pull this off in an established village where infrastructure is already
built and residents' lives are generally settled. But the potential for
conflict is certainly greatly enhanced by the state of flux that results
from the constant infrastructure projects that Sanctuary still has to
accomplish. Disputes over cutting down trees for solar access for
farming and renewable energy, and the aforementioned dispute over
building legally or not have raged through Sanctuary and tested its
commitment to consensus. Even the commitment to consensus has
become a large enough issue to be a contributing factor for some ex-
members' leaving. Nevertheless, the hope, at least among advocates
of consensus, is that a continued dedication to this process will over
time develop a deep connection and trust among residents, and potentially be a transformative example to other communities after a few
decades of success. There's certainly no doubt that through consensus
each member feels that they have a political voice. The problem is that
they may have too much of a voice, a single vote potentially delaying
or blocking progress, turning the process into a tyranny of one rather
than an agreement by all. It will certainly be interesting to see if Sanctuary is able to continue this commitment as they move forward. I,
for one, would not be surprised or, truthfully, terribly disappointed, to
see it abandoned. The purity of consensus certainly is attractive, but
expediency is also important, as all of our time is limited. I would hate
for the whole experiment to fall apart instead of them implementing
some kind of majority-vote or perhaps consensus among elected rep-
resentatives type of system.

For building and other major infrastructure projects such as rainwater collection, plans must be approved beforehand by a Sanctuary
committee, but builders also face the additional question of whether
they will get their building approved by the county. Whether to try
and get the building or other project legally approved by the county

inspector is left to the owner (all land is held in common, but individual buildings and their accompanying infrastructure are privately owned). Inspectors are wary of alternative materials such as cob and straw bale, especially since these have yet to make it into the Universal Building Code, the bible of most county inspection offices. But inspectors are also hung up on having an automated heat source to keep a residence at 63°F. The basic worry, as far as I can tell, is that if the owner is away during the winter the pipes could potentially freeze and cause massive structural damage once they thaw. Passive solar heating is completely disregarded in this context, and of course water doesn't freeze at 63°F. Besides, it's a simple thing to put in a drain to empty out a home's pipes. It may be hard to convince an inspector, but homeowners actually care if pipes break and cause massive structural damage. When faced with such nonsensical criteria that potentially forces homeowners to install very costly fossil-fuel based automated heating, Sanctuary allows residents to opt out of getting a Certificate of Occupancy from the inspections department. Likewise, architectural drawings and an engineer's stamp, assuming they could be obtained for alternative building methods using natural materials, green roofs, greywater recycling and rubble trench foundations, are also often prohibitively expensive. There's a wealth of knowledge available for new residents who are building, not only in the existing buildings but in the folks who built them, many of whom still reside there. So probably the most important enforcement mechanism that ensures the building complies with Sanctuary's accepted criteria is the visibility of the project and the trust that other village dwellers have in their vetted new neighbors.

The major written enforcement mechanism that Sanctuary employs, whether for complying with stringent ecological integration for new infrastructure or for regulating other antisocial behavior, is called the Gradual Series of Opportunities (GSO), formerly the Gradual Series of Consequences. The last of these consequences is physical ostracism from the community (which hardly seems like an opportunity to me, so maybe they should have stuck with the former name). But long before that happens, the community tries to work with the individual or family to change their behavior. One cited example when the GSO was enacted was with a junky yard with high visibility. The resident had also built several smaller huts for people to stay in, that were unsanctioned by the building committee and against the rules. From what I could tell from talking to folks, the GSO was not being terribly effective in changing the behavior of the recalcitrant individual. The case seemed to languish for years without any major improvement, causing ill will. So in many ways Sanctuary and its political structure raised more questions than it answered. Basically, they're still trying to figure it out, and fortunately the place retains an air of dynamism. They are on the vanguard of trying to radically reorganize everything about daily life, and you don't figure out such gargantuan questions in 15 years.

It was enlightening to contrast my visit to Sanctuary with a few days at The Farm, a more traditional hippie commune from back in the day. The Farm sits on several thousand acres just outside of Summertown, Tennessee. For decades I'd heard tell of this famous commune from other like-minded social misfits and the occasional random former resident. When I was 18 and traveling by Greyhound I'd met another 18-year-old who'd grown up there, and his back-of-the-bus tales of freedom from the travails of The Man had piqued a lifelong interest. Finally, I had the time and an excuse to visit and see what all the hubbub was about. There aren't too many pockets of radical hippiedom left, and the fact that such a place had survived for four decades in the normally conservative southeast United States was certainly intriguing. What was there to learn from such stability and perseverance?

Admittedly, my notions of the place were colored by talking with folks, especially at Sanctuary and our peak oil group, about more recent intentional communities. I went there to chat with Stephen Gaskin, the guru and founder, and Albert Bates, author of the influential *Climate in Crisis* (1990) and prominent intentional community activist, who moved there a few years after its founding. Unfortunately, Ina May Gaskin, Stephen's wife and pioneer of the midwifery movement, was out traveling. How did more recent efforts to build sustainable communities contrast with what went down back in the early '70s? What kind of trouble did such a massive undertaking confront back then?

The first notion I was disabused of was the idea that The Farm was intentional. It took a good part of my conversation with Stephen to understand the difference in attitude that accompanied the founding of The Farm back in the late '60s-early '70s from a place like Sanctuary, formed in the mid-90s. For the folks who started The Farm, worldwide revolution was imminent, as was a massive reorganization of everyday thought and everyday life. The Farm would be a revolutionary seed that would end world hunger, instigate world peace and bring enlightenment and contentment to all who lived there. When I asked about the decision making process in selecting the location and how they planned to function politically when they started, Stephen

I couldn't help wondering if this was one of the original school buses on the round-the-country tour that founded The Farm. No one seemed to know.

just gave me a blank stare. A genial man, he however appeared to be a tad miffed at my question and lack of knowledge of their history. Finally he said, "There was no decision making process! We just needed land enough to park 50 buses full of 1,500 hippies!"

The Farm started out as a traveling speaking tour for Mr. Gaskin, who had built up a devoted following at San Francisco State College during the late '60s. His Monday Night Class, as it became known, became swollen with students and nonstudents alike, reaching 1,500 attendees on a weekly basis. Feeling that the revolution was too localized and that the good vibes of San Fran were being ruined by hard drugs and criminal miscreants, he took his gospel on the road, to all 48 contiguous states. A large number of his students came with him, and they picked up more on the road. Mr. Gaskin spoke at a lot of churches, using his magnetic personality to connect with local preachers who were concerned they were losing the spiritual ear of the youth in their flock, and who wanted to understand what all the hippie hullabaloo was about. I have a thing for garishly colored old school buses turned into mobile housing, and it never fails to bring a smile to my face to imagine small-town America being overwhelmed by the cacophony, visual tumult and general anarchy that must have ensued each time this caravan rolled into town. Asked if there were any confrontations with the law, Stephen gave me one his sly looks, and said "Every time!" The first thing he had to do was reconnoiter with the local law enforcement and try to figure out if there was a nearby park or farm where his clan could stay. Some times this went well, other times it didn't, but by this point they were a force of nature. One or two small town cops were no match for 1,500 hippies.

Towards the end of the speaking tour, Stephen wanted to parlay the energy it had created into something long term. Being on the road for so long had many hardships — spending lots of money, eating crappy food, bus breakdowns, toddlers not in school, etc. So when some land became available 60 miles south of Nashville, he directed the caravan there. They would build a new society based on love, peace and understanding, and then take the revolution to the far corners of the globe.

Albert Bates' handcrafted solar electric go-cart for motoring around the farm, parked in front of his house.

To some extent, they succeeded. They're still there, after all. And The Farm still boasts outreach programs in Central America, the focus of much of its international charity work. There are viable businesses, ranging from mushroom spawn cultivation to radiation detector manufacturing. Although not the 1,500-person goliath commune of yesteryear, after 40 years 150 still call The Farm home, with many ex-residents nearby. It's hard enough to imagine creating a successful town with diligent planning like what's gone into Sanctuary, but how has The Farm been relatively successful, and what were those early days like when a bunch of citified idealistic kids tried to make their way on the land? One great account of those early days is in a collection of first-hand stories from mostly former residents describing the travails of building Eden from scratch, called *Voices from The*

Farm. There were many fuck-ups and even some near death experiences, perhaps the most hilarious of which is when a couple of folks tried to take down a nearby large water tower to move to The Farm, nearly killing themselves in the process. Another great one Stephen told me was about curious neighbors sneaking over in the woods to watch naked hippies sow seeds in an open field. The image is idyllic to the point of hilarity, the voyeuristic rednecks, probably in camouflage, nestled in the leaves for an afternoon's entertainment. I'm not a farmer, but I can imagine that trying to grow and harvest grains in the buff turned out to not be a very successful endeavor. Unsurprisingly, trouble quickly brewed with the law over some reefer being grown on the property. Three residents were arrested, and Stephen, as spiritual leader and dedicated pothead, also took responsibility. After a drawn-out court battle, Stephen had to spend one year of a three-year sentence in the pen.

This moral stance seems to have solidified Stephen's role as guru, and despite his absence actually provided some cohesion to the nascent community. Part of what made The Farm successful was this guruhood. Much of the community possessed an idealistic faith in Stephen and his teachings, and his martyrdom provided additional impetus to continue on with the project. If you're of the opinion, as I am, that such idealism on that broad a scale is unlikely to be replicated anytime soon, what pertinent lessons are there to take away from The Farm's early history? I think the primary lesson learned was The Farm's transition from outlaw commune to a successfully integrated village by working with the existing county political system, despite widespread interference from the federal government, especially the FBI's efforts to financially ruin the endeavor. Residents of The Farm got involved in the surrounding community. Especially during the more populated early years, they were able to tip the balance in a southern county that was transitioning from being historically Democratic to Republican. They stopped growing pot and started attending county commissioner meetings, and even tried running for office. Politicians, including the sheriff, had to come to The Farm and get votes. Residents moved out of buses and teepees and into homes they built that the local inspector could recognize as dwellings and make legal. The effect this integration had over the years was perhaps something of a loss of identity. Stephen's role as guru dwindled as residents matured and tried to find deeper answers to the hard questions of life, and as his humanity reasserted itself and the idealistic glow of that age ebbed. When I interviewed him in 2010, he was 75 years old, and parked in his bed in front of a gigantic television set that he seemed loathe to turn off. He came off as a wonderful, funny and generous man, but I was having a hard time imagining committing myself in any way to him as my spiritual guru. Maybe that's just cynical old me.

In my mind The Farm made a catastrophic error that will keep it from ever thriving as any kind of village in the future. It's too spread out. Many residents use cars, or at least golf carts, to get to different areas like the small health food store, and especially to run into Summertown for supplies. It is, ultimately, a sprawled-out suburb, and the private homes fail to create a public space that anyone would recognize as a nice place to walk around or just be. Even though the homes are built ecologically, this lack of cohesion into a public space means that, like all suburbs, it fails to integrate itself into either the human or natural community, something that James Howard Kunstler pillories so cogently in his books like *Home from Nowhere*. Whatever revolution was once going on here has definitely moved on, and it's heartening to see a place like Sanctuary learn from these lessons and strike out in a bolder redefinition of what a sustainable village could look like. The law may not be with Sanctuary yet, but the spirit of inquiry and revolution is.

4

Alternative Architecture

I GREW UP IN THE BURBS, a no man's land of boxes and highways. We lived in a box, we rode around in shiny metal boxes, even time was divvied up into boxes. Bells rang and I moved from one classroom box to another, listening disinterestedly to prepackaged lessons until the lunch bell rang. Then I went to an enormous box and ate food made out of cardboard. A few more boxes of time and then I got on a giant yellow box and rode back to our box, where I would kill time watching a flashing box — Three's Company, What's Happening, Alf.

I would ride my bike around our neighborhood, where the most prominent feature of most homes was the garage for the automobiles, a style of building I would come to call "carchitecture." Out front, a few small bushes would be the only green thing around, usually openly hostile holly bushes with spiny leaves that would attack you if you scraped against them. Even these bushes were shaped into boxes.

Growing up in a family where my father and three brothers were all variously employed in engineering, the built environment was of incredible importance to me. I am a builder by nature. From my teenage years, I had an overwhelming desire to build my own home. When I got together with my first wife, we also had a strong desire to escape what seemed to be the empty and destructive existence being lived by our elders. At that time, there was little philosophy behind this motivation, more just a visceral instinct that what we witnessed around us was built on a rotten foundation. Building our own home would turn out to be an almost decade-long process, one that would be a long education in society's rigorous reinforcement of the status quo and its ignorance and often outright hostility towards sustainable alternatives.

By our early twenties, we had used a small inheritance from my grandparents to purchase 10 acres of land about 45 minutes north of Durham. Our education in alternative architecture had begun. At first, our primary motivation was thrift. Once the land was purchased we had very little money to build much of anything, especially after putting in a well, septic and driveway. What could we build to live in by using materials readily at hand? How much reused stuff was available? What would be inexpensive to operate in the long term? Coming from a land of bigger is always better, McMansions and SUVs just starting their hostile takeover of society, these were radical thoughts.

At that time in the mid-90s, there was very little evidence of alternative architecture, although a powerful new movement was just starting to bubble under the surface. Much of what we came across was either the traditional pioneer building styles such as log cabins, or relics from the 60s and 70s, some of which we soon discovered we wanted nothing to do with. We had a good friend who lived in a geodesic dome, built in the mid-70s a few miles outside of Chapel Hill. It was a fascinating place, and the roundness of it was appealing, at least up to a point. There was a little mini-dome built beside the original one, its function never entirely clear to me, but cute as the dickens. Both domes leaked like sieves, of course, and although a dome does enclose the largest volume of space with a minimum of materials, just as Bucky claimed, much of that space is utterly unusable. The walls slope inward at about waist high, and are curved to boot. So pushing furniture against the walls was impossible, leaving mice superhighways behind. No one who'd ever lived in the dome had ever figured out how to insulate the thing, the triangles that made up the ceiling not being amenable to any of the rectangular board insulation sold at the lumberyard.

The easiest way to become an outlaw is to go out in your yard and build something. Pretty much whatever you build will be illegal. When we first got our piece of property and I talked with the health inspector who was okaying our septic system, I mentioned we might just cut down some trees and build a log cabin. After a penetrating stare deep into my eyes to see if I might be a crazed psychopath, she mentioned that was impossible, unless I hauled the trees to a registered sawmill and had them kiln-dried and stamped. Wouldn't they be just as dry and stable if we dried them out for a summer out of the rain? Yes, but they wouldn't have the stamp from the mill, and without that, no legal abode. It seems that nothing is more threatening to the powers that be than trying to live in something other than a balloon-framed, Sheetrock-encrusted box. Surely doing so will result in your early death and the withering away of all that is holy, or so you would think to listen to the average inspector tell it.

As we studied alternative building styles and I learned more about its history from the '60s onward, I became fascinated with radical building the way a young boy does with Billy the Kid and John Dillinger. I got my hands on a copy of Mike Oehler's *The $50 and Up Underground House Book*. Very little heating or cooling costs and integrating the home so well into the surrounding environment that you couldn't even tell it was there? Underground homes were where it was at! During this time I went back to my folks' house to visit and the surrounding woods were being slaughtered to make way for more houses. Their subdivision had been one of the first in the area, and a great part of its charm was being surrounded by untold acres of beautiful woods where a young boy could roam and escape the confines of boxland. Now the woods and the topsoil were gone and red clay ran like blood down gullies into the creek I had loved as a child, the beavers and turtles long gone.

A copy of Lloyd Khan's *Shelter* cracked my mind open much further. The idea of indigenous architecture salved my builder's soul, so badly damaged by the murder of my boyhood forest by giant fossil-fuel-powered dinosaurs building unsightly boxes using wood from clear-cut Canadian forests. A copy of *Woodstock Handmade Houses* given to us by a friend left me itching to get blisters on my fingers, but now there were so many ideas I was paralyzed. Hilariously, the cover of that book features an orange behemoth made out of spray-foam insulation and looking like a giant turd shat by an angry god (it did blend into the surrounding environment with a sort of Rabelaisian flair), but other inspiring homes inside the covers mixed reuse with natural materials in a thought provoking and creative way.

In September of that year, 1996, we restarted school at the University of North Carolina at Chapel Hill, recently married and stuck in my parents' basement since we hadn't yet figured out what to build. A dome still seemed like the one default option that had any hope of being legal. Then a fierce hurricane whipped up from the coast and plunked a big pine tree on Dan's mini-dome, which seemed propitious. At the time we were investigating and preparing to have contractors build a concrete monolithic dome. This was some sort of compromise, I suppose, between the fascination domes still had on us mixed with our suspicions about their longevity and practicality, combined with any inspector's lust for all things concrete. Maybe the hurricane should have reinforced our desire for the monolithic dome, since our contractors claimed it could withstand a direct hit from a tornado, but its permanence made building one seem irrevocable, and to our unsure minds, still bummed we hadn't figured out a legal home we could build ourselves, we dithered until the opportunity (and enough money) passed. The rigors of school beckoned. But not before we'd laid a giant round concrete foundation 32 feet in diameter, looking like some kind of helicopter pad or roller rink out there in the woods.

It was starting to get cold. We needed a home. Specifically, one that was round, cost less than five grand and could be built in a couple of weeks. Turns out there is, in fact, such a thing: a yurt! Throwing our hopes for legality to the dogs, we made the purchase from Blue Evening Star, who hand-sewed the yurts out near Sedona. She claimed it was the biggest yurt she'd ever made, the biggest one she'd ever heard of. Usually they were no bigger than 30 feet in diameter. When our yurt collapsed under a record snowfall a few years later, we'd understand why.

In a few weeks we had our yurt cover, and in the interim we had been working on making the lattice-work that would form the cylinder of the structure. If you're not familiar, a yurt consists of two separate parts. The base is a series of lattice-work, in our case pine 1×2s purchased from the big box lumberyard. The lattice-work is stretched out to form a short, squat vertical cylinder, meeting at a door. At the top of this lattice-work, a cable of some variety is woven. Our cable was braided steel wound through the pine 1×2s. A cone is then plunked atop the cylinder by notching rafters into the cable and attaching them to a hub at the top of the cone. A cover is then stretched out over the cylinder and then another atop the cone. In place of much more traditional and romantic yak-skins, we had some variety of vinyl with a few tear-dropped shaped windows around the hub. Even for a yurt this large, that leaves only one means of egress, something that perpetually nagged at me once we lived in it. We would build raging fires in the wood stove to try and keep the leaky thing a few degrees above the outside temperature, and I was forever wondering what the flash point of the mysterious vinyl covering was as I nodded off to sleep.

The idea of a yurt is that it's semi-nomadic, but this point gets lost when you're building one 32 feet in diameter on a giant slab of concrete. Precariously balanced on a flimsy aluminum ladder on top of some hastily put together scaffolding, trying to balance the heavy plywood hub on my head and attach at least three of the rafters so that the hub (and myself) wouldn't plummet to the ground, it occurred to me that if the inspector showed up at that particular moment and tried to reconcile what I was doing with the building plans for a small conventional cabin we had submitted earlier that year, I would be in deep shit. Our flirtations with legitimacy, pursued in earnest up until that point with a half-dozen or so strained conversations with the building inspector, had come to an abrupt end. In our minds, we continued to tell ourselves that the structure was only "semi-permanent," to rationalize, I think, our ultimate discomfort with building an illegal home.

In the end, it didn't make it to "semi-permanent," staying firmly in the "just temporary" timeframe. People don't build yurts that big for good reason, especially the flimsy way we'd built ours. As per instructions from Blue Evening Star, which didn't, I don't think, take into account the absurd size of our yurt, we had ripped 2 × 6s lengthwise to form the rafters. Of course, actual 2 × 6s are really 1.5 inches by 5.5 inches, meaning the end product was less than 3 inches deep. The 2 × 6s were 16 feet long, and when you rip a long board like that in half lengthwise, all of its funkiness and squirreliness comes out. There wasn't a straight rafter in the whole thing, but fortunately there were lots of them. Everything about our yurt was over the top. The hub held up by all those twisted rafters was 14 feet in the air. We lived in a giant circus tent that flopped around in the wind, something that would become a major problem when we tried to insulate it by shoving sheets of 4-feet by 8-feet blue board styrofoam insulation between the rafters. With the sheets of insulation in place, every slight movement in the wind would create hideous squeaking noises, and when it really blew, the apocalypse was nigh.

If the inspector had shown up while I was up on that ladder, he might very well have saved us from the attempt on our lives that the yurt later made. But he would also likely have snuffed out my long and amazing adventure in underground sustainability that was just starting to (literally) pick up wind. It's fun, in your youth, to see how little you can live with, what extreme conditions you can endure, to brag to your friends about how tough you are. I'll never forget being huddled up under thousands of layers of blankets and reaching over in the middle of the night to get a sip of water, only to be denied because the water in the glass was frozen solid, despite the raging fire I'd had going just before bedtime. May I never experience such horrors again!

Once spring arrived, there was only one thing to do: throw a party! We were twenty-three and owned ten acres of woods and a yurt; it was the only sensible thing to do. At that age, we still had all the wildness of youth with little of the responsibility of adulthood, despite our being landowners. We invited all our friends out for the weekend and had bands play, despite not really having a functioning toilet, legitimate electricity or a kitchen sink. It was a very wild time, with lots of marijuana smoking and nudity, but of course it's not really a wild party unless firearms are involved. Some friends of ours had hacksawed off a giant giraffe head from a bankrupt putt putt place in Raleigh. On Easter morning, as we all shook off the second morning's hangover, they set up the giraffe head in front of a pile of clay, pulled out a couple of shotguns, and blew the poor thing to smithereens. There was nothing redeeming, constructive or sustainable about this, but it was damn fun.

We managed to finish college living in the yurt. Then we had the brilliant idea of moving to New York City so we could "use our degrees." It was a mostly rough year and a half where we worked too much and drank too much, but we did manage to save up a good chunk of money, always with the idea in the back of our heads that we might move back to the land and build a real house.

We escaped from the city just before Y2K. Remember those times? Not that we thought the city was going to go up in flames around us, but just the same, it was good to be out of the rat race, at least for the present. A good friend of ours ran a website called Y2Ktimebomb .com, preaching the gospel of industrial society's imminent ruin. But the calendar turned, and life went on.

Soon after the new year, we traveled to Mali in West Africa with our friend Andy, who'd been finishing up his PhD at Carolina and living in our yurt. We had a mutual friend, Nathan, stationed there for two years of Peace Corp. This was an amazing place to be as we recovered from our stint in the city and started to turn our focus back towards building a home in the woods. We stayed for two weeks with Nathan in the remote village of Djallakoraba. Could there be a greater contrast to New York City, where everything is steel boxes stacked upon concrete boxes all the way up to the sky? I doubt it. The serene little village, without phone, without money really, consisted of groups of homesteads plopped haphazardly around one another, each composed of a series of modest round, earthen huts with thatched roofs and decorative plasters.

Upon our return to North Carolina, we started building our cob home, inspired by what we saw abroad. Unbeknownst to us at the time, we were following in the footsteps of lots of other experimenters from around the country who were taking their building inspiration from indigenous earthen architecture from around the world, and who, like us, desired the buildings they constructed and occupied to represent a transition between themselves and their environment. Modern conventional building seeks to be standardized, square, interchangeable and maintenance-free. It is architecture for a nation of deracinated refugees who expect to receive nothing of substance from their homes, and who likewise wish to offer nothing in return to them. If Megacorp, your employer, tells you your job has moved from Charlotte to Tacoma and it's time to pack your bags and go, this isn't a problem. There's a home waiting for you there that is just as banal and sterile. You'll hardly notice the difference, or care, and the home's modern systems and materials likely won't require any of your attention — until their 20-year warranty is up and they need to be replaced.

Indigenous architecture contains a sense of place, and it is this sense of place, this rootedness, that is the radical departure from the way we live now. It also requires attention, care and interaction. Just like relationships with living things, the more time you spend taking care of something, and it you, the deeper the bonds that develop. Maintenance is the basis for caring, so it's not surprising that our maintenance-free architecture is also "care-free," i.e., no one gives a shit about it. One of the amazing things that has developed in the alternative and natural architecture movement is that we creative North Americans have taken traditional styles of building from all around the world and infused them with playfulness. If maintaining one another is the basis for caring, playfulness goes one better. It is the food of love.

Not only does natural building require maintenance, much to our benefit, but it's also possible *to* maintain it, and to do so with materials readily at hand. While building, and while maintaining, the land becomes the home. We don't buy things from a big store and then put them together. We cull them from the surrounding land and *create* them. Our buildings are the land, just rearranged to our desires. The more we are able to play with our buildings, and with our land, the more we are able to create buildings we fall in love with. A positive reinforcing cycle develops. The more we love our buildings, the more we enjoy caring for them. Playfulness generates beauty, beauty inspires us to care, and caring means longevity. Perhaps more than any other ingredient of sustainability, longevity is of primary importance.

This is the difference between platinum LEED-certified whatever and a natural home, built by someone local with as many indigenous components as possible. Natural building, because it is part of the land and requires us to care for it as it cares for us, roots us. Because it is amenable to non-specialists like owner-builders, and because it can incorporate organic forms, its range of playfulness and beauty is much greater and deeper. We are able to fall in love with these buildings, and thus also the surrounding land that they are a part of and represent.

Garden House, one of Sunray's latest creations and where he currently lives with his wife Bonnie. The house is built with a mix of cob, stone and local lumber.

Created from the land and the builders' inspiration, they are utterly unique. This uniqueness creates an awareness that is fundamental to making us feel alive. It is no wonder that The Man is so challenged by any of us trying to live in anything other than a Sheetrock-encrusted box. Alternative architecture allows us to gain independence by not needing the big box hardware store, to care for our buildings and land, and to not want to be an interchangeable moveable cog in the industrial corporate machine.

This playfulness was on amazing display on a visit to Sunray Kelley's spread, outside of Sedro-Woolley, Washington. I've been involved in natural building for over a decade, and I've seen what I had considered to be a great variety of inspiring forms and creations of cob, stone and unmilled wood. But I was about to have my socks blown off by the intricacies and natural engineering talent of Sunray's structures. The man himself is a work of art, stout and handsome, always barefoot, and with a bedraggled, dreadlocked graying beard cascading over his shirtless torso. When I arrived mid-morning, he was seated with his wife Bonnie at the kitchen table, finishing his morning coffee and toking on a Cheech and Chong-sized joint. He offered a gravelly welcome, a large bowl of kind bud in front of him on the table like a dish of porridge, as Bonnie fixed us a cup of joe.

After he regaled me with some highly entertaining stories of run-ins with the law as a youth, the sunlight streaming through a porthole window behind him, Sunray and Bonnie gave me a tour of the property. Sunray works shoeless, and his left foot was maimed from a recent encounter with a chainsaw while harvesting some posts. He limped over to an old tractor, the massive cut unbandaged and his foot swollen, and fired it up, slowly puttering down a gravel lane as I ambled behind him, the single cylinder engine punctuating the silence of the morning with its gasps.

Sunray's place is a large spread of family land, where he grew up with his parents and brother. An innate builder, he started his first home soon after high school, using materials from the woods and hillsides he played in as a child, a resource he referred to as his "super natural market." This was the early '70s, and this part of Washington is logging country, so the obvious thing to build with was wood. But whereas the corporate behemoths were interested in denuding the land of every tree in sight and making as many board feet as possible, Sunray harvested trees selectively and judiciously, often with an eye for using the most unique and curvy wood available, parts of the forest that the box-makers would only scoff at. Of course, building with organically shaped wood is much more difficult than slapping together some two by fours into a balloon frame, and his sculpting skills were as important as his carpentry. Nature loves roundness and hates rectangles. Corners are weak points that eventually cause buildings to fail. The inherent wisdom of evolution has never produced a tree with a square or rectangular trunk. So using unmilled wood is an inherently sound practice, even though the lack of uniformity drives inspectors nuts.

One of the hazards of working barefoot is putting a chainsaw into your foot. Sunray hopped aboard an old tractor to give me a tour of the property.

Sky House: four stories of curved wood standing proud in the forests of the
Cascade foothills.

A half dozen or so homes were spread out across the hillside. Being an innate builder can be a curse. I speak from experience. It can
be impossible to stop creating. After you complete one home (or almost complete it — the final details seem to always get forgotten), you
end up always thinking about how cool the next one will be, how you
can incorporate everything you just learned into something better.
Likewise Sunray has never stopped building on his property. He has
created a mini-village of inhabited sculptures. Now many of them are
rented out, meaning all types of folks get to live in works of art, no
matter their profession, and Sunray has some retirement income as
age has made him less able, as it does us all.

Since many houses were rented out, we only got to go inside the
oldest home, called Earth House, of which Sunray was especially
proud and thus didn't mind imposing on its occupants with a tour.

We intruded on the friendly couple who lived there, with me oohing and aahing at the lush interior as they nervously followed us around, obviously anxious for us to leave so they could get on with their day. Honestly, I was too enraptured to realize how rude I was being. As with Sunray, it's been the case with other builders I've met and visited over the years that their first home is often the most spectacular, even though the methods may still be crude. This is, I think, a combination of two things. First, the chronic underestimation of how long unusual forms and fancy details will take, especially when using organic materials, which are then often neglected to save time in later buildings. And second, the unbridled enthusiasm that makes every owner-builder believe that this first work is going to be the most amazing house ever. In Sunray's case, that's not far from the truth.

We approached a curved, wooden, arched doorway, covered in mossy split-cedar shingles, that revealed an elaborate diamond-shaped stained glass window sitting atop a sculpted, thick wood door. Inside, the house was centered around a main chimney with four fireplaces, with naturally curved stairs leading up to a loft above. The home is in part a self-portrait of Sunray. His carved face sits above one of the mantles, and four hands come off the center posts to hold up the main roof rafters, as if parts of his body had been physically

A detail from the interior of Sunray's first work, Earth House, conceived partly as a self-portrait. Here a cast bronze hand extends from the main fireplace column to hold up a roof rafter.

incorporated into the structure itself. There is an overabundance of wood, which gives a dark and brooding aspect to the interior, as if you were hunkering down deep in the forest itself to escape the ravages of modernity. Sunray seemed disappointed with the lack of natural light in the building, and confessed to not understanding the importance of passive solar when he built Earth House. A slanted-glass greenhouse had been added to the south-facing downhill side of the building, and on this beautiful sunny August day, you could feel the heat wafting up the doorway into the main part of the house, not unwelcome up in this northern latitude even on a summer day.

In the '90s, after Sunray had been introduced to cob by Ianto Evans of Cob Cottage down in Oregon, he incorporated this organic form of masonry into his preexisting curvy style. The combined playfulness of these two natural forms is sometimes overwhelming at first, lending an almost carnival atmosphere to his structures. This exuberance is enhanced by retaining branches and even leaves on the

An exterior staircase from an outbuilding. Continuing his organic style onto even more prosaic buildings gives the entire "village" a magical and integrated feel.

unmilled posts that jut cattywompus from the roofline. By leaving more fragile parts of the tree on the rafters some decay is inherent in his buildings. The leaves fall off and many of the smaller branches eventually break off. In a sense the buildings are never complete, because they are designed to accept the idea of reincorporation with the surrounding environment from which they came, at least up to the point where it doesn't interfere with structural integrity (depending on proper maintenance, of course). Granted, I wasn't talking to an unbiased source, but it seems that the structures have held up well over time, despite their artistic whimsy, though I couldn't help wondering. I was reminded of the quote by one of Frank Lloyd Wright's clients who, upon hearing her new home was leaking three weeks after completion, reputedly quipped, "That's what happens when you leave a work of art out in the rain!" Pushing the envelope as far as Sunray does probably means some perplexing maintenance and water issues for these homes down the line, but the inventiveness they exhibit and the joy they inspire certainly seems worth it for now.

It was great to get the grand tour from Sunray and hear all about his building methods and philosophy. He was one of the last stops on my cross-country tour, and I was beginning to detect a common early life history among all the amazingly diverse people I was visiting and profiling — that of the misspent youth. It seems like almost all of these sustainable rebels had gone through a wild period in their late teens and early twenties where nothing terribly creative was happening yet but the foundation of mistrust for authority was clearly blossoming. Of all the tales I heard, I think Sunray had one of the most amusing, especially given his skills as an innate raconteur, and I think it's worthwhile to recount it as a paragon of the adolescent restlessness and rebellion that seems to typify this unique type of activist.

Just when his first major house construction was beginning, back in 1973, Sunray was driving around with his brother Tim, going the usual 100 miles per hour with pot smoke pouring out the windows. They were coming back from a family reunion in Utah, just near Colfax, Washington, when Tim was pulled over by the cops. Tim got shuttled into the back of the squad car and Sunray had to follow him to the station. Once inside, the police decided they wanted to search the car, but Sunray wasn't having it, knowing there was a big grocery bag of reefer in the back seat. So he headed for the door, but before he knew it there were a half dozen deputies piled on top of him giving him the full treatment, including a fat spray of mace right in the face. They threatened to charge Sunray for destroying their uniforms and, of course, found the reefer, enough for a felony charge. His mom came and bailed them out and a suppression of evidence hearing for illegal search and seizure went nowhere.

Heading into the court room for trial about a year later, Sunray spotted a deputy walking in ahead of him with a very familiar brown paper sack. Determined to take back what was formerly his, he ran up, snagged the sack of weed, and bolted down the stairs, the unamused deputy and several other lawmen on his tail. As he burst out through the courthouse doors, confused jurors watched from the window of the cafe across the street as he fled. He was a spry young lad and outfoxed the cops, hiding the bag of pot in some bushes before he returned to the courthouse for trial, fully expecting the case to be dismissed for lack of evidence.

No such luck. Instead he was indicted on grand larceny, obstruction of justice, and a second felony count of possession for the same weed! The newspapers had a field day in the morning edition, priming the pump for Sunray's notoriety. He was eventually convicted of both counts of possession. The other two charges were dropped, but this was still enough to get him a year's stint in the state pen. This turned out to be not so bad. Security was lax, and Sunray spent a lot of time with his brother Tim hiding out on the branch of a tree smoking smuggled pot. Then he had a big break, getting work detail building a picket fence for the Department of Natural Resources. Attention to regulation being lax, he was able to convince DNR to deliver extra unwanted lumber and wood to his house construction project back home. When he finally got free, most of the lumber he needed to finish building was there waiting for him. Perhaps it was this serendipity that allowed Sunray's whimsical style to fully bloom. Regardless, the good news is that they got the bag of pot back!

5

Art

I'VE BEEN GOOD FRIENDS with artist Matt Bua for the better part of two decades. I was first introduced to Matt through a mutual friend, the sometimes rock star and general shape-shifting poet Ryan Adams, a close friend during my tumultuous teenage years. Fresh out of high school in the early '90s, Ryan and I lived together in a crumbling four-bedroom shack of a house on the west side of Raleigh, North Carolina, where we would stay up all night drinking forties of cheap malt liquor and collaborating on puerile "novels" that contained no verbs, banged out on cheap old typewriters, our creativity occasionally supplemented with overconsumption of cough syrup. Late one night, on an impromptu caffeine-fueled jaunt, we headed down the dark highway towards eastern North Carolina and ended up in Matt's college town of Greenville, home of Eastern Carolina University, in the wee hours of the night. Ryan had previously met Matt through the pre-Internet underground web of alternative music, art and literature that survived mainly through late 20th century zines like the Xeroxed rag *Lark's Tongue in Fluke Juice* Matt helped put together with a friend. Despite the fact that it was four in the morning, we decided to rouse Matt from his bed.

We threw rocks at Matt's window until we finally saw his head poke through under the sash. Regardless of the hour, he was happy to see his old friend Ryan, and invited us in. It didn't take me long to realize that, coincidentally, I had recently submitted a poem to Matt's zine, and our friendship took off from there. From then on, I would trek down to ECU whenever Matt had an art happening, until he wrapped up his art studies in Greenville and made the move to New York City to make his way as an artist.

Matt's art has, since that first night, been expanding my understanding of what art is and what it is for. I had a fairly traditional education when it came to art, usually taking the word as just a shorter way of saying "painting." So once every year or so, I'd have my mind blown when I'd make it up to New York City for an opening and to see what Matt (often working with his collaborator Jesse Bercowetz) was up to. A recreation of the Mir space station built using found objects (and inhabited for days at a time by the artists); drawings made by attaching a pencil to a U-Haul moving truck and driving it back and forth; a long-term commitment to beef up by lifting weights and then performing a coordinated exercise routine in freaked-out jumpsuits for crowds of onlookers — those are just a few of the many projects that Matt and Jesse had going on. Other contemporary work in their circle of friends included an artist living inside the walls of the art gallery for a month, or focusing on "transmission art" such as radio wave manipulation and attempts at free energy through Tesla coils.

After a dozen years in the city, Matt broadened his focus. After purchasing property in the Catskills near Hudson, New York, he starting setting up a place for art to interact with its surrounding ecology through small buildings, a project he calls "b-home." Buildings and the environment — these are things that are right up my alley and I was happy to pitch in some time to help get him started. I didn't have to spend too much time up there before I starting getting my mind blown again, not just from the loose structures Matt was throwing up, but also by the buildings his collaborators were putting up, and then by the multifarious dimensions of other eco-art being creating nearby and all over the world. While artists probably hate to be labeled more than anyone, I'm going to go ahead and risk getting in trouble by referring to Matt and other artists experimenting with nature as eco-artists.

On my latest trip up north I detrained in Hudson at 2 AM. Outside the station, I saw Matt's ancient but mostly intact Ford F-150, easily capable of squeezing at least four people in the front seat, come rolling down the hill through the dark fog. I jumped inside and rambled through the winding hills to b-home.

I awoke the next morning in a structure called the Owl's Den to brilliant September sunshine, the sugar maples just starting to show a hint of vermillion and the forest floor covered with protruding mushrooms, some of which we knew would make their way into the night's supper. b-home is located on the western side of Vedder Mountain, and is split in two by a power line cut. From the road, the property is entered from a small ridge and slopes quickly down to a modest brook, around which most of the current activity focuses. Coming down the slope, it doesn't take long to realize that the normal world of rectangular buildings and organized grassy lawns has long since been abandoned for a different paradigm. Immediately at the bottom of the hill, a large metal storage container leans northward, its contents spilling outward down the hill towards a plexiglass-roofed structure that looks like it barely survived a Japanese earthquake.

This marks the beginning of a long allée lined with the discards of American civilization, from piles of rough-cut lumber, storefront

Civilizational detritus collected from New York City and a defunct local sawmill ready for transformation into artistic mini-buildings at b-home.

totem poles, and rolls of plastic tubing to fellow artists' homeless art projects like a giant barbed-wire teddy bear and a functioning corn liquor still. Beyond these piles, what appear at first glance to be crudely built hobbit dwellings on closer inspection turn out to be intricate structures of indeterminate use, their organic geometry comprising an unexpected wholeness. In many of these small buildings, natural elements like multitudes of branches wrapped together, earth plasters and living trees are integrated with manufactured items such as randomly-cut sheets of metal and plastic, children's action figures and old windows. The immediate impression is of the work of a flock of giant bowerbirds that raided the remains of Fresh Kills landfill and then headed north into the mountains to build their empire. It almost goes without saying that such structures would not enjoy the blessings of any conventionally-minded inspector, a point Matt chooses not to dwell on for any great length of time.

This is a retreat from the confines of everyday civilization, but not the kind where you get to lounge around poolside in the sun. With its goal of changing how the civilized world conceives of its relationship with the natural world through the medium of the built environment, the work at b-home is never-ending. Since there actually isn't any flock of giant bowerbirds, the hard work gets done by Matt, his girlfriend Laura and the migrating rotation of artists and builders that come through.

Most of my work this visit centered around building a human-scale solar oven to keep Matt and Laura warm in the brutal winter months. Using six posts that Matt had sunk deep into the ground on a south-facing hill and secured using a packed-rubble footing, we created a triangular building of perhaps 100 square feet, the broad side opening towards the winter sun. A solar oven works by creating a small, black, well-insulated space that can be dramatically heated up using reflectors to capture the energy of the sun. The goal of our building was not to cook the contents, of course, but rather bring the wintertime temperature up from subzero to a living temperature of around 60°F or 70°F.

For backup heat storage and as a means of supplemental heat, we worked hard building a high-thermal-mass rocket stove. A rocket stove is a unique kind of masonry stove. The basic principle of both is to create an extremely hot fire capable of combusting almost all of the smoke, making for a very efficient and clean burn. Instead of this heat immediately warming its surroundings, it's stored in a substantial amount of masonry such as stone or brick. The heat then percolates out into the surrounding room over a period of 12 to 24 hours. What is unique about a rocket stove is the design of the burn chamber. Instead of having a traditional fire box, wood is burned vertically from the bottom. The heat and smoke are then captured momentarily in an insulated truncated chimney covered by a metal barrel, where the temperature rises high enough (upwards of 1,200°F) to complete the final combustion of smoke and other particulates. The heat from this chamber then winds through masonry before exiting the building. In our human solar oven design, we planned on the rocket stove heating a bed made out of cob, to keep its inhabitants warm through the long, cold northern nights.

The usual daily routine at b-home involves many of the ecologically minded activities I'm used to back home: putting a dinner dish

Matt's "Lower-case a-frame" humanure shack, where business gets taken care of.

in the solar oven, hunting in the woods for goodies like Cinnabar Chantarelles and Chicken-Fat Suillus, emptying out the humanure buckets into the compost and checking the meter on the PV system. It's not just the art itself that's ecologically minded; the life lived in its creation is as well.

The ecologically minded art and lifestyles at b-home are part of a reinvigorated movement to interpret our myriad ecological dilemmas through the kaleidoscopic lens of art. It is the duty of the artist to act as both mirror to society and as thought-provoking visionary of what might be. With their recognition of our inability to maintain our civilization in its current guise, it's not surprising that many artists today are incorporating ideas of ecology and sustainability into their work. Artists have always been on the margin and underpaid for work whose value might not be recognized for years or decades (if ever), but eco-artists like Matt who are embracing ecological issues

A cascading cordwood sauna at b-home with a loft upstairs to take advantage of residual warmth and a widow's perch for a good view of the stream.

are nevertheless remarkable in the contemporary art world for the almost universal unmarketability of their creations.

Whether it's rows of genetically modified corn being "taught" about civilization, a giant decaying bunny rabbit, or an abandoned war vessel turned into a model of sustainability, these works are often conceptual or site specific and hence inherently unconsumable as art, something that would make Dabl proud. Their difficulty in making eco-art into a commodity is perhaps the one common trait all eco-artists share. By frequently incorporating discarded items that everyday folks consider garbage, the first message their art conveys is perhaps the primary tenet of sustainability: *there is no such thing as waste in nature.* Or more succinctly still: *don't waste waste!* One creature's discards are often another's fundamental source of sustenance, whether it's the leaves of a tree in fall, the excreta or carcass of a mammal or the alcohol left over from a yeast's consumption of carbohydrates. Likewise, eco-artists often make use of the discards of industrial civilization to show that today's one-way street of production ➛ consumption ➛ waste should be replaced by what Linda Weintraub, author of several booklets on eco-art, describes as a more "cycle-logical" or "eco-centric" vantage point. Cycle-logical refers to a psychological mentality that thinks in cycles, and eco- replaces ego- to focus our collective consciousness on habitat rather than self. The two terms neatly summarize the change in outlook that eco-artists attempt to engender and that Ms. Weintraub documents in her books like *Cycle-Logical Art: Recycling Matters for Eco-Art.*

My adventures in understanding art's relationship to nature were expanded still further with an invitation to enjoy breakfast at the home of Portia Munson and Jared Handelsman, nearby neighbors and friends of Matt's. Nestled at the base of a mountain on the edge of Catskill State Park, the two hundred-year-old-home has been in Portia's family since the 1930s. After a delicious meal of scrambled eggs, fresh from chickens I could see wandering around outside the huge picture windows of the breakfast nook, I was treated to a grand tour of the property and a peek inside this fascinating couple's evolving philosophy about their art and its shifting relationship to the physical natural world they inhabit.

Credit: Portia Munson

Portia Munson's *Stargazer*, one of her recent flower mandalas created from flowers from her home garden. Portia's artwork encompasses everything from "trashscapes" to these more natural arrangements.

For a long time art has been divested of its sense of place, and it's this divorce from geographical identity that today's crop of eco-artists is struggling so hard to repair. Like much of the rest of industrial civilization, modern art in the twentieth century suffered from a homogeneity that made its message equally valid hanging in the studio where it was created or on the walls of a CEO's office in Tokyo or Los Angeles. In this sense modern art implicitly had as its core theme the rootlessness of our industrial existence. Portia and Jared's work centers around their home and its daily and annual rhythms.

Portia first made a splash in the art world with her monochromatic accumulations of plastic detritus arranged in "trashscapes" that reflected our cultural assumptions back at us through their vastness. In *Pink* (1996–99), you are bombarded by the submissiveness suggested by the little girl connotations of all the pink plastic. From Barbie dolls to fake cosmetic containers to miniature kitchen setups, the overall effect is an undeniable domesticity and incompleteness due to some missing (presumably male) presence. She expanded on this mode of cultural introspection with *Green* (2007). This color has two strong, divergent meanings, envy (and probably not coincidentally money) versus sustainability or environmental. The irony of the latter of these two meanings is instantly conveyed by the huge agglomeration of plastic crap, much of it manufactured in China, whose poisonous presence will be felt for eons as the junk, mostly toys functional for perhaps a few years before some fragile plastic part breaks, will take millennia to photodegrade into bazillions of itty-bitty plastic nurdles that will disrupt the hormones of ocean-dwelling fish almost into eternity. Even the idea of envy or greed is neutralized by the utter undesirability of all of this broken junk.

As Portia became more settled in her Catskill mountain abode, her artistic attention shifted to the garden outside her front door. She began to take notice of the cultivated flowers that still showed up every spring, planted by relatives long since passed. Here was an unnoticed familial connection transported through time by the rhythms of nature. She began imagining mandalas of arranged flowers and started laying these out on a scanner. She often slices into the flowers and fuses buds together, or cuts them open to reveal their interior anatomy, letting the pollen fall on the scanner's glass like sand.

Matt and I finished up our coffee as Portia concluded her truncated descriptions of her artwork, needing to get busy with her day's activities. I was dying for a tour of the property, having been informed

One of the suspended stone sculptures that Jared Handelsman created deep in the woods on the property he shares with Portia Munson.

by Matt before we headed over that Jared had lots of crazy sculptures scattered around the nearby woods. At the risk of being a complete pest, I got Jared to start us on the tour by asking to see his blueberry spiral, visible through the windows of the breakfast nook and the focus of much of his landscaping energy of late. The ploy worked, and Jared was soon leading Matt and me on a several-hour tour of not just the giant blueberry spiral but also the huge historic barn they had moved over a decade ago from down the road and reconfigured into their studio space, some maple syrup boiling operations, a treehouse hovering over the nearby creek and Jared's previous efforts at landscape art that his modesty and evolving philosophy had made him less than enthusiastic about.

Jared's background was as a sculptor, and once he and Portia moved into their Catskill abode his artwork initially focused on slightly altering the landscape around their home to emphasize the organic patterns revealed where two separate natural materials met. Typically, this meant using large steel cables to elevate a large section of bluestone slightly above its original place to focus the viewer's attention on the relationship between the stone's natural home and its surrounding environment. Jared was very interested in site-specific installations as opposed to the large hunks of steel his art education had emphasized could be placed or "plopped" in any generic location: in a museum, in front of a skyscraper in New York City, etc. This lack of a sense of place and belonging that characterizes much of twentieth-century sculpture is alluded to derogatorily as "plop art." To its critics, plop art has nothing to teach us about where we belong in the world or how to interact with our surrounding ecology.

Poppies, a more recent photogram that captures the play of light on these flowers, and avoids creating some of the "visual pollution" of Jared's earlier sculptures.

Credit: Jared Handelsman

But Jared eventually tired of this method of site-specific work, even though I found it thought provoking as we meandered from suspended giant rock to suspended giant rock. Jared had begun to consider his sculptures "pollution," and it took some needling to get him to explain what he meant by this term. I didn't feel like his alterations had negatively affected the attractiveness of the woods in any substantial way, but Jared now thought that the pieces, like perhaps all sculpture, were just visual noise and disturbances that detracted from the woods' inherent beauty. He now focused his artistic attention on making photograms, or long-term exposures of photographic plates to various natural and man-made light sources. One of his favorite sources of artificial light is the headlights of cars as they curve along the road in front of their house at night. Jared's deepening respect for his surrounding environment had led him to abandon sculptural work altogether, and turn instead to documenting the play of light on his property. But for someone like me who is still a novice in understanding how ecology-based artwork can reveal deeper relationships between humanity and nature, his older pieces still had a strong effect. After we piled back into Matt's F150 and returned to b-home, I had a new appreciation for the lines of connection that naturally arose between all the living things and the stone and ground they sprouted from.

Interview Questions for Matt Bua about the b-home Project

Q: What is the purpose of all these small buildings scattered about? Are they meant to be habitable in any fashion?
A: Once it has a roof over it and the person stays dry in the rain, the first goal is reached. The next is make it bug free, then warm.

Each structure has a different purpose. The sauna is both a place to sweat and due to the large dug-out rock which the stove sits on, is the coolest spot during the hot months. Some structures will act as permanent tents, but built with more resilient material that does not break down in sunlight like plastic does. Some are merely roofs over an old stump to slow down the decaying process because I like the way it looks.

I have this saying "roof it, then poof it." Quickly get the roof on so as to protect it, then let the interior develop slower. If someone visits for a few days, they can take an unfinished structure, put in some screens and windows and have a nice place to sleep and read. As Constantin Brancusi said, "Architecture is inhabited sculpture."

Q: It seems like you have an eclectic selection of building materials in various piles out here, from what look like discarded totem poles to rough-cut lumber to rope crafted from discarded plastic bags. Where does all this stuff come from?

A: The two different sources are rural upstate New York and New York City. Since no one has storage space in the city you find a wider range of material, like theatre props, thick Plexiglas with fashion ads on them and lumber from disassembled lofts. Whereas upstate, you can get pine, cedar and oak off-cuts from the mills, as well as discolored boards with lots of life in them from defunct mills.

Many pieces of my past art projects/structures have found their way up to be integrated into upcoming buildings. Other artists have offered up their art where it can live on, free from the jaws of the landfill: Allison Weise's *Whiskey Still*, Rachel Lowther's *Orange Wolf*.

Q: Tell us more about some of your collaborators on this project? Did they start from a similar artistic/sculptural background as you did?

A: Jesse Bercowetz's structure is the first building I had no hand in. He mentioned he was demolishing a Chinese gadget store's warehouse and we loaded the material in the truck and brought it up. A day and a half later there was a ski-haus/bridgekeeper's inn. One wall is complete, door jambs, hinges and all, stacked horizontally. It's much more urgent than the other buildings since he was hell bent to roof it before the day's end. He had to come back and do a little emergency triangulation to give it a little bonus stability.

Carrie Dashow's *Archive of Lost Thought* is built completely from downed trees left by the power company. I engineered the overall structure which Carrie is now in-filling with a chaotic wattle and daub mud/cob which will enclose the centrally located pit kiln. I keep trying to talk her into making it the Swiss army knife of kilns, meaning let's make it cook pizza, smoke fish, make tar and maple syrup, but she wants it to solely fire the participants' clay objects that they've instilled with their lost-thought energy.

Q: What do you envision as the ultimate aim of b-home? Will there be other artists or architects permanently based here?
A: I see it as laboratory for trying out as many building techniques as possible. Keeping the sizes small will hopefully prevent "Giant Dream House Syndrome" where people get bogged down with trying to make an oversized castle that is impossible to complete. b-home will produce small structures which then can be installed in public venues and used as necessary, such as bus shelters, pallet saunas, compost toilet pods or a giant animal form/mascot building for select towns. The stockpile of materials will be utilized by others to develop their own prototypes for building systems. The possibilities are wide open.

Q: What is the definition of Visionary Architecture? What are some of the other thinkers and designers in this movement working on?
A: The classic definition is "paper architecture," ideas that remain unbuilt on paper. As we see though, without Archigram's drawings and ideas (author's note: Archigram was a group of avant-garde architects active in 1960s London), the Pompidou Center would not have been created. Groups like the Small House Society and Architecture For Humanity are giving people the push to realize their ideas in down-to-earth functional ways. Sure, Rem Koolhaas can make a giant bird's nest for China's Olympics, but it's Mockbee's Rural Studio that is empowering people to get involved with the building process and engage the communities. There's the design/build mentality taught at schools such as Yestermorrow whose goal is to push people into action by showing them that it can be done in realistic ways that don't include a 30-year mortgage and monster houses that consume tons of fuel and energy.

So I wouldn't call what I'm doing Visionary Building, but more like Intuitive Building…reacting to different terrains, materials and functions. As Constance Adams says, "If you can't visualize it, don't build it."

Q: One thing that stands out here is the beautiful natural setting on the western slope of Vedder Mountain, and how you've integrated so many different types of man-made materials with natural ones, even living things like trees. The juxtaposition of the natural and the man-made is striking, and seems to reflect the property itself, which is bisected by a clearcut of power lines. What message are you conveying by this juxtaposition of different materials?

A: At first, I was in awe of the land, all the rocks and trees on it. I also had no chain saw. So when I sited buildings, one or two trees able to continue growing through them seemed fine, they were here first. In fact it was the tree growing through the library that held the structure up after it took a direct hit from a large pine tree that went down during the heat wave microburst of 2008. The two quotes I think of are Frank Lloyd Wright's: "Make the house 'of the hill,' not 'on the hill,'" and Bernard Rudofsky's: "There is much to learn from architecture before it became an expert's art. Untutored builders…demonstrate an admirable talent for fitting their buildings into their natural surroundings, instead of trying to 'conquer' nature."

The act of melding these wide range of materials together becomes just a puzzle-building game.

Rather than following plans to a "T," you're reacting to the developing being's wishes and whims, creating a sculpture that you inhabit at the end and enjoying the surroundings.

As Claude Levi-Strauss wrote in *The Savage Mind*:

> There still exists among ourselves an activity which on the technical plane gives us quite a good understanding of what as a science we prefer to call "prior" rather than "primitive" could have been on the plane of speculation. This is what is commonly called "bricolage" in French. In its old sense the verb "bricoleur" applied to ball games and billiards, to hunting, shooting and riding. It was however always used

with reference to some extraneous movement: a ball re-
bounding, a dog straying or a horse swerving from its direct course to avoid an obstacle. And in our own time the
"bricoleur" is still someone who works with his hands and
uses devious means compared to those of a craftsman.

Q: How do you think this mixing of man-made materials with a natural environment will impact the ecosystem here over the long term,
especially when these man-made materials such as plastic begin to
break down and become potential pollutants?
A: It's all a balancing act. On one hand it's a celebration of entropy,
watching nature rub shoulders with the newly built additions, while
on the other hand trying to build for long term. A lot of getting my
hands on as much high quality roofing material to keep the weather
out and know the building will be here for a while.

Also the learning curve is slowly happening where before, pouring
concrete in with pressure-treated poles was the only way I thought a
post foundation should be. Then I learned of the rubble and rock in-
fill with landscaping cloth and instead of the pressure-treated wood, I
can use oak or black locust.

I'm paying close attention to plastic and how much sun exposure
it gets. The structures planned for the top of Mt. Vedder will be logs
only, mud chinking, slate roof and maybe wool insulation. Since
everything must be carried up, it will all come from a 500 foot radius
from the building site.

Q: The overall ethos here seems to be very ecologically minded. Some
of these structures serve as toilets in a simple cartage-based humanure
composting system, the electricity comes from solar panels, much of
the food is cooked in a solar oven and comes from an organic garden
or wild foods found on the property, like mushrooms. Is this ecological thoughtfulness a fundamental character of visionary or intuitive
architecture, or just an incidental component of it here?
A: It's all a slow process of getting the most out of the land and working with what it has to offer.

I've never gardened in my life. So trying to plant as many hardy native species that will come back year after year seems to be most appealing. After I chopped a big oak down for the first time, I felt I should use this amazing tree for all it's worth. Smaller branches for railings, trunk pieces for building posts, if any of it is used for firewood, I want to get the most out of it by heating the most insulated structure possible. I'm constantly looking at my trash thinking, "What can you do for me in the future?" I would much rather build with it today, than drive it to the dump.

Q: Do any of the artists in residence here ever squirm about shitting in a bucket and hauling it to the compost pile later, or eating wild foods or bathing with rainwater?
A: Everyone reacts differently. Sometimes the light instantly clicks on in people's heads: "Yeah that make sense." Others keep it to themselves and never come back. The longer people stay, the more the land weaves its spell of plenty. The intern last year arrived not knowing what a green pepper or zucchini was, living on donuts and Fruit Loops, and left a milkweed and fiddlehead addict.

Q: What about the legality of what goes on up here? For instance, the uninspected buildings and the humanure composting, which are subject to zoning and construction regulations in many places. If the building inspector showed up unannounced one day, how would you defend what you've built up here?
A: I like to say the most important law is, "Don't piss off the neighbors."

In reality I did introduce myself to the code enforcer and she okayed the 12 × 12 cabin plans. Factors such as it not being a year-round living quarters and my primary residence being in NYC put the structures in a different class. As with the composting, with a little research you can find out the safe distances from water, and how to properly do it. Any visitor will hopefully see my goal is to be a good steward of the land.

6

Marijuana Cultivation and Alternative Medicine

A s the health care debate raged in the first part of Obama's presidency, I remained deeply skeptical about whether our goliath health care system could continue to function in a coming world of industrial scarcity. Of course, I want everyone to be healthy, but the atomized nature of Western civilization's approach to health seems incongruent with a well-functioning, sustainable society. It's typified to me by the changes in my town over its history. Durham has gone from an economy focused on tobacco to being a self-described "City of Medicine" today. It's important to note that we don't describe ourselves as the "City of Health," because there's simply no money to be made in healthy people. What kind of economy or city would that be? A bunch of folks exercising in the sun, eating fruit off trees, walking and biking around, just being healthy? Ain't no coin in that.

So with one hand we make you sick, and with the other we sell you medicine. Eat too much here, take these diet pills over there. Buy a car and drive around, but then pay to ride an exercise bike at the gym. Eat fast food and drink gallons of soda, then go to your doctor for your heart disease and diabetes. Whatever you do, just make sure you keep consuming more and more so the economy can keep growing and make everyone better off.

When I first conceived of this chapter, I wanted to focus on alternative medicines such as herbalism and how they butt heads with this archaic method of thinking and the laws in place that reinforce its dollar-oriented paradigm. I'd had my own unsuccessful history of growing American ginseng on the wooded land surrounding our cob home, spending several days in the late winter of a few consecutive years raking aside leaves, sowing the persnickety stratified seeds in the rich humus, and then covering them back up and hoping for rain like any other good farmer. Our property in North Carolina's piedmont was just on the edge of ginseng's natural range, a bonus in the sense that the crop is frequently stolen during its seven-plus years to maturity and there were thus no likely poachers. But while the plant grew well at first, voles and several hot dry summers eventually did much of it in without any help from two-legged thieves. My interest in natural medicine waned as other pursuits like natural building and renewable energy took off, but over the years I had made the acquaintance of three herbalists and was hopeful they might be willing to participate. While my book project seemed to pique their interest, when it actually came time to set up a meeting during my travels and get their story about how natural medicine might butt heads with conventional health care law, the inbox of my e-mail and voice mail remained empty. They were, I suspect, busy wandering around in the woods, and who could blame them. It reminded me of the behavior of one of my favorite musicians, Django Reinhardt, the three-fingered gypsy jazz guitarist who would frequently skip scheduled performances to go take walks on the beach. I would be remiss to think that wandering around in nature is less important than my own book project, so my feelings weren't too badly hurt.

During these missed connections, a somewhat related opportunity presented itself that I couldn't resist — the chance to visit some pot-farmers in the mountains of the Emerald Triangle (Mendocino, Humboldt and Trinity counties) in Northern California. On some level the two topics of psychotropic drugs and herbalism are intertwined, but less so, I suspect, than the rhetoric of marijuana pro-legalization advocates suggests. This was something of a tangent, but it was definitely illegal! And reefer raises its own interesting questions about sustainability beyond its potential as a potent medicine, because it gets you high, and whether it's coffee, alcohol, tobacco, pot or something else, almost all of us like to get high. So I asked a different question: What is a sustainable buzz?

I've long had a low subsurface guilt about consuming coffee grown in faraway tropical lands. This hasn't stopped me from drinking a few cups a day and truly enjoying the hell out of it, and I hope it never will. But if the global economy really did fall off its rocker, I suspect acquiring real coffee would become too dear, and I'd be left drinking some bitter chicory concoction that might not suffice to get me out of bed in the morning.

Coffee's not my main gig, though, beer and wine are. Beer is easier to justify, with a good selection of local brews in my hometown, and a brewery dedicated to some crazier concoctions like sweet potato lager just a block from my house. Despite the breweries being local, the grains and hops are all coming from far away, and of course there's all those fossil fuels to cook the wort. I homebrew erratically, sometimes on my wood stove or out in the backyard with my rocket stove, but the aforementioned brewery a block away keeps tempting me away. Wine is another story. Despite one or two dozen North Carolina vineyards, I'm enough of a snob and the wines are expensive enough to keep me from patronizing them with any regularity. And the wines I buy from California and Europe are not very nearby, so there's that low-level guilt thing again.

And then there's pot, by most accounts North Carolina's biggest cash crop, larger than tobacco. I've always been fascinated with this drug, but I generally find its high overwhelming. In my early twenties I became very interested in growing it. There was a drug war on, and you have to choose sides in a war, right? I was on the side of drugs, at least natural ones like reefer and mushrooms. It also seemed like a promising career choice in addition to my ginseng growing. I lived out in the sticks, and was surrounded by clear-cut forests that seemed like the perfect disguise for a few well-placed patches of the noble herb. A like-minded friend and I cloned some choice females one spring and started readying the soil in our clandestine locations, deep in the overgrown briar patch. This involved hauling many 40-pound bags of cow manure and mushroom compost through rough terrain. It was great exercise. I was in great shape.

Man, did those plants grow! I tried not to visit them very often, but when I did, I was awestruck by their vitality and mystery, even though some were deer-chomped. Something about the idea of a plant being illegal was so ridiculous to me, when I'd visit one of the patches and see those liberated ladies, I was just so proud of myself and what I was doing. And I was going to make a lot of money! Everything was going swimmingly.

Until one day, in early September, just as they were starting to tip over with the weight of their buds, they were gone. We weren't sure exactly who'd snagged them, but it looked like a big operation. The whole area was a mess, broken branches everywhere, and they'd been pulled up by their roots, so Johnny Law was the primary suspect. What a bummer! My buddy and I later learned a tried and true saying about growing outdoors. For every patch you want to harvest, you have to plant four: one for the deer, one for the neighbors and one for the cops.

We tried a more guerrilla approach the next year, choosing a somewhat more overgrown area deeper in the clear cut, sacrificing some sunlight, planting only a few plants in each patch and spreading them way out. It worked. We brought in a good quantity of pot that fall, made some money and a lot of hash from the trimmings, and starting dreaming about next year.

The next year was very dry. Even with hauling five-gallon bags of water in a backpack through the brush in the searing early summer heat, horseflies and mosquitoes attacking me the entire way, the plants were barely growing. To compound matters, we'd got a late start on the clones and so had an abbreviated growing season. Still no rain came, and the thermometer was pushing 100°F almost every day. I loaded up the pack with the heavy-ass water one afternoon and started on the journey. I made it to the second patch and was giving some relief to the thirsty ladies when I heard a rustling in the brush. I stopped watering and listened. More movement and soft crinkling of leaves. Oh my god, it's the fuzz! They've staked out my patch and I'm going straight to jail! I didn't move a muscle, not sure if I should high-tail it or sit still. Why hadn't they busted me yet? Maybe they didn't know I was here, but that barely made sense. I looked into the thicket of brambles and saplings, but couldn't see a thing.

I heard a very loud sneeze and then a riotous commotion. I was sure I was being charged by a half-dozen cops. I was terrified, and it still baffles me to this day how I didn't shit my pants. But instead of the boys in blue, it was just a few deer galloping away through the brush. Our white-tailed deer make a kind of sneezing sound when startled. I'd heard it many times before, but had mistaken it for a human sneeze. I was safe. After a few minutes to calm myself down, I finished watering and got the hell out of there.

A few weeks after that, in the late afternoon, I was taking a bucket bath in the yard after a muddy day of plopping cob on our house proj-ect, when I heard a helicopter approach. It came closer and closer, until it hovered just a few hundred yards away. I stood there in the buff, wondering what the hell they were doing. It was just at the tree line, but I could make out the entire 'copter and even see the pilot. Then it clicked. It's hovering over my pot patch! It had seemed so far away and deep in the woods when I walked there with 40 pounds of water on my back, but as the crow flies, apparently, it was less than a quarter mile away. Then I got worried. There weren't many houses in the area. It probably wouldn't take much deduction on their part to guess that the pot plants were somehow associated with the wet, naked hippie living in a yurt and building some other structure out of mud a quarter mile away.

What to do? I talked it over with my former wife, and our first inclination was to get in the car and go somewhere, anywhere. But that would just make us look guilty, right? I got dressed and threw the stick for the dog, trying to act casual as the helicopter hovered. It must have been there for half an hour. We stuck it out, cooking dinner and watching a movie that evening, waiting at any moment for The Man to show up. But nothing ever happened.

A little more than a week later my curiosity got the best of me. Did they find *all* my patches? The likelihood of them staking out any of the patches in the searing July heat seemed thin. I snuck my way over, now actually feeling like I was in an honest-to-goodness war. When I finally made it there I did a big loop around the first patch to try and flush out potential enemies. No sign of anything. I took a deep breath and made the dive in through the brush to the patch. The ladies, of course, were gone. All that was left was a business card from the local sheriff. The same scenario played out at the other patches. My weed, and my pot growing career, had come to an end.

It has been over a decade since these adventures, and I still carry a special place in my heart for those mysterious ladies, so elegant in bearing, yet so naughty in nature. When that chance connection allowed for a visit to some professional growers in Northern California

Relaxing with a cold beer and some beautiful ladies in Humboldt county.

on my cross-country trip, I couldn't wait. It would be mid-August, meaning their plants would be full grown and likely just starting to flower. It was a very interesting time to visit politically as well. Proposition 19 was on the ballot that November, basically an attempt to change marijuana in California from its "medical" status to outright legalization, something I am very much in favor of generally.

Apparently, not many residents of the Emerald Triangle were in agreement. I say "apparently" because I was not introduced into the larger reefer community in the area, and received most of these opinions second-hand from my hosts. Pot is very big money in California, around $14 billion annually. The vote represented a very real economic threat to the entrenched growers up here, threatening to wipe out a way of life.

Before you get all misty eyed about eco-minded hippies in the hills losing their small source of income and no longer able to buy farm implements, tofu and solar panels for their geodesic domes, please know that those days are long, long gone. The big boys have moved in, most of the pot is grown in underground grow rooms that burn tons of planet-fouling diesel to power artificial lighting, and they use their millions in easy profits to drive around in Hummers and build garish McMansions tucked back in those same hills where the flower children once roamed. Gun ownership probably approaches 100 percent. I was vociferously warned to obey property boundaries on the few short meanderings I took among the California black oak and dry grass. It didn't take me long to circle the perimeter of known safe lands and realize I was, to all extents and purposes, trapped on my hosts' compound in the same way I would be in a minimum security prison. I couldn't *see* the men with the guns, but they were there.

Other than that, the area is an idyllic paradise. Winding mountain roads provide amazing views of fog-shrouded valleys where the redwoods grow (or used to) to towering heights. Some of the sunsets up there would make the gods themselves quiver with delight, with the Pacific Ocean a felt but rarely seen presence just beyond the iridescent ridge tops, so vast it's capable of absorbing the totality of the sun in its waters every dusk. I know, I know, you don't want to hear me

A typical greenhouse set-up for growing this "sustainable buzz" that by convention keeps curious copters at bay.

wax poetic about sunsets, you want to hear about the ladies! Well, the ladies were lovely. Fortunately my hosts had the decency to be outdoor growers, definitely old school in their retrofitted solar-powered octagon home, although outdoors actually means in hoop houses or other obscured greenhouses so the helicopters can't "know" what's in them. This all goes back to some arcane court ruling that basically says that simply having a greenhouse is not suspicious enough grounds for a search warrant, but the interpretation is constantly in flux based on an almost continuous docket of cases coming through the system, and whether the presiding judge is more friendly towards the growers or the feds. Regardless, any actual law enforcement seems to come in periodic waves and mostly only affects the really big growers. My hosts explained what variety they were growing, although honestly I can't remember well, something like a hybrid cross of Kush, Bubblegum, and AK47, or some such nonsense. It doesn't make much difference to me, since the high from all these different strains of potent ganja all feel like getting hit over the head with a crowbar as far as I can tell (in a pleasant way, of course).

So, okay, pot is basically as easy to grow as cabbage, but when you buy it, of course, it costs a thousand times as much. Growing and consuming this drug should be a cheap and fossil fuel-free enterprise. Instead, it has turned into a goliath industrial enterprise and attendant prison complex that is sickening to behold. If pot were legal, I could pretty much grow enough in my fifth of an acre city lot, if I wanted to, to keep my entire small city stoned (assuming no one steals it all — a pretty big assumption). One full-grown plant can put out two or three pounds of dried buds, so if we assume about 50 potential highs per ounce, that's somewhere in the neighborhood of 2,000 per plant. Any way you look at it, when it comes to getting high, pot is by far the most sustainable buzz. At least it should be. It can be grown locally almost everywhere in the world. It can be naturally dried. Transportation costs are nil. With all these great things going for it then, why did 850,000 Americans get arrested in 2009 for possession, costing roughly 10.7 billion dollars in taxpayer money, to say nothing of the ruin it inflicted on these many individuals? Is this just another example of our capitalist growth economy in action?

Making pot illegal creates a lot of jobs where otherwise there wouldn't be any. All those "offenders" have to be locked up, see their parole officer, take re-education classes, etc. The growers up in Humboldt and the rest of the Emerald Triangle have to pay for underground grow rooms, artificial lighting, diesel fuel, fertilizers and pesticides, etc. Then of course they go and buy Hummers and McMansions with their profits.

This seems like the obvious answer, and I'm sure it's a big part of it. Our society seems to value one goal above all others, so it's not surprising that freedom, fairness and a carbon-free buzz would get trumped by the megalith of relentless economic growth. But I also strongly suspect that there's a more fundamental reason to pot's perpetual illegality, and that's the nature of its high. On my six-week journey visiting all the radical and amazing people I've been profiling, the waft of marijuana smoke was a near constant companion. As you might guess, folks who have no trouble breaking the law to adhere to their ecological beliefs also had no compunction about using an illegal plant for their altered states of consciousness. Not all partook, but many did, and it was partly this psychedelic consistency that motivated me to include this chapter on weed.

In my experience, alcohol generally tends to make situations more tolerable than they might be otherwise. Its most famous role is as social lubricant, allowing its users (like myself) to overcome their introverted tendencies and socialize with greater ease. It alleviates boredom. Sit me in a chair in the sun in the backyard and I will be amused for ten minutes, but keep bringing me delicious pints of lager and I will likely stay there all afternoon perfectly contented (until I pass out in the dirt and wake up a few hours later with a pounding headache). It's often possible to drown miseries with a few stiff drinks. Alcohol lets you not pay attention.

Pot, on the other hand, and again I'm speaking from my personal perspective, *forces* you to pay attention. Your normal routines and daily rituals, your ingrained thought patterns and assumptions about the world — reefer takes a giant eraser and scrubs all these out for the duration of its high. (Okay, probably a little longer than that.) You have to reconstruct almost everything that you do or say, find a reason or meaning for every action. If you want people to accept and follow a bunch of rules at face value, *this is a very dangerous thing!* Chronic pot smokers don't necessarily seem to be affected in this way. Occasional users often find this experience to be unpleasantly overwhelming. A big part of the reason it is overwhelming, though, is because of its illegal pariah status. Pot, like all psychedelics, is heavily dependent on setting and mood for the quality of its experience. By making potential occasional users feel like outcasts who might get locked up with a bunch of murderers and rapists at any moment, the authorities are essentially able to ruin the high for most people. By breathing paranoia into the experience and thereby making many folks have a bad time, they can then reinforce the general opinion that it is a bad drug. Fear prevents any reevaluation of our consumerist soul-sucking culture by most occasional users. At the risk of sounding like Timothy Leary, I think part of the path to a sustainable society can be accomplished by some good old-fashioned pot smoking, freeing up our brains for a much needed questioning of the many, many dubious and downright false assumptions we have made about the world. Let me also be the voice of moderation here and say unequivocally that partaking with too much frequency seems to be as damaging or perhaps more so than not. My favorite analogy to any kind of psychedelic experience is that of traveling. While a few trips a year (*not* speaking metaphorically here) can greatly broaden the mind and allow you to contrast a different way of life with the one back home, a life of constant wandering with no sense of place is a life lost. Traveling is a form of taking, where you imbibe the culture and creations of others for your amusement and edification. What have you done for the travelers who visit your home? Have you helped make it a place of beauty and community? Granted, there are periods of our life where such inward-seeking constant travel is required to find our sense of self and place, but it should not become a lifelong endeavor.

Some of the nonsense of pot's illegality came back to tarnish the travels of a pair of hitchhikers I picked up at the beginning of my trip in North Carolina. I left the Firefly primitive gathering (more on this in Chapter 8) towards the end of July with three fellow travelers packed into the Saturn wagon, a young couple in their early twenties heading out to Colorado to work on an organic farm, and an intrepid if somewhat goofy young man named Zach, 24, working his way back home to Portland, Oregon. The poor wagon was packed to the gills with backpacks and tents as we lumbered through the southern Appalachians, but I was happy to return a karmic favor that I'd been granted on many occasions when I was a similar age. I was taking this motley crew as far as St. Louis, at which point I was veering north to Chicago. We all interviewed Stephen Gaskin together at The Farm in Tennessee, and I knew I was working on the right book project when bringing three scraggly hitchhikers along for the interview did not reflect poorly on my professionalism, but rather enhanced my credibility.

In St. Louis we all crashed at an acquaintance's house and starting planning our separate routes. Zach had done a fair amount of train-hopping and I had been picking his brain about it. It's always interest-ing to meet and talk with someone who pretty much holds identical beliefs as you do but takes them much further. For me, this is saying something, because I often feel like the radical eco-nut in any mixed gathering. But Zach's integrity in all things ecological was hardcore. Back in Portland, he biked everywhere, never had a car, and dump-ster dived a large portion of his food. He also gathered lots of food from fruit trees and gardens, trying to limit his harvest to produce with some imperfections or that otherwise seemed abandoned. What really captured my imagination was his hoboing on trains. There's extra space on those huge empty trains, he told me, why not jump on and get a free ride? I was intrigued, until I heard the details. Rather than riding in a boxcar, protected from the elements, the easiest way to hop a train was to jump on a particular type of grain car that had an extra, generally empty bed in the back of the larger storage compart-ment. Here, an enterprising hobo could snuggle up and travel hun-dreds and even thousands of miles across the expansive West. Zach did much to make this sound romantic in the extreme, laying under the stars as the train puttered along at 15–20 miles per hour, the huge Rockies dissolving into the gloaming as the infinite lights of night slowly revealed themselves.

But the nitty-gritty of it sounded a little less than appealing, espe-cially to a fellow in his mid-thirties with a creak or two already in his bones. The hard steel container becomes viciously cold in the clear mountain nights as the thermometer plummets, and the constant rattling and jarring makes it almost impossible to read or otherwise concentrate. And, of course, it does sometimes rain, even in the arid West. At which point you get chilled and soaked right down to the bone. Train-hopping is illegal — you're trespassing on private prop-erty, and if you're caught you're probably going to spend a night in the clink (which, honestly, sounds much more pleasant than being in a cold metal jumble box of a grain car). I am a lover of trains, and I've even hopped a few back in my teenage years for a few miles at a time, but I'm going to stick with Amtrak, as lame as that can often be. The number of routes are, admittedly, much fewer than for commercial train traffic, but I'm stuck at a level of required comfort above the very low-carbon lifestyle of a hobo, much as I would like to be otherwise. Zach didn't hesitate, however. He received some pertinent train-hopping info from our hosts (it was that kind of crowd), and within two hours of showing up in St. Louis was down by the tracks, sneaking past security and continuing on with his clandestine voyage back home.

The other pair of hitchhikers, who I'll call Marissa and Mike, were sticking to the more conventional method of sticking out their thumbs on the vast interstate system (Eisenhower's great military-industrial gift to our nation) to get where they were headed, which has its own legality issues, depending on the state. Ironically, I was actually going to the small podunk town of Paonia, Colorado, where they were heading to work on an established organic farm called White Buffalo, Paonia being the headquarters of Solar Energy International where I had some interviewing to do. But I was Chicago-bound first, slowly meandering my way there, so we parted company.

I called and left a message once I arrived in Paonia a week and a half later, but I got the feeling by the lack of rings on their cell phone that they were out of range of that modern convenience (not a hard thing to do in southwest Colorado). I had wanted to catch up and perhaps visit the farm they were working on, so I was a little bummed, but that's the way it is when you're traveling — lots of chance encounters that make the trip interesting and then life rolls on. On Friday, the last day of my week in that most pleasant little burg, I was driving around doing some grocery shopping for a dinner party some friends were throwing that evening. Who should be slowly strolling down the road in front of the beer and wine store but Marissa and Mike. I recognized them easily from a distance — a tall man with a long glowing orange beard and cut-off jeans, and a spunky, almost bantam-sized girl nearly half his size with long brown hair, apparently wearing the same clothes as when I'd dropped them off by the entrance ramp to I-64 in St. Louis almost two weeks before.

I pulled over and we exchanged hugs and hellos. "How's it going?" I asked, and found they had both rapidly tired of the voluntary slavery of farm interning. "We want to go to California and get trim jobs!" they told me. At first I didn't understand, but then they explained there was good money to be made trimming and manicuring reefer buds, the harvest apparently just getting underway in sunny California. So like so many generations before them, they had made up their minds to head west and find riches in that beautiful and enigmatic land. I wished them luck. I was heading that way soon myself but, honestly, I was not able or interested in taking them on as fellow travelers again. I assumed this was the end of our acquaintance.

A few months later back home in North Carolina, I received an urgent e-mail from Marissa asking for a character reference and a letter stating that she had been traveling with me during the summer. They'd found their trim jobs, but they'd been busted, and the strain of it had ended their relationship. Granted I'd only spent three days with Marissa, but those were three days in a tightly-packed Saturn wagon driving cross-country, and you get to know people pretty quick under such intimate circumstances. To think that this poor young vivacious and intelligent girl would potentially have to spend a year in jail for her cursory involvement with a pot farming operation was preposterous. I was happy to supply her with the necessary document, and she did eventually manage to extricate herself from the criminal charges and return east to get on with her life.

In our wasteful society there is a huge amount of low-hanging fruit available to easily pluck on our way to a more sustainable civilization. Probably the lowest fruit on the tree is replacing coal-sucking tanning booths with solar energy — go get your tan in the sun and save the coal! But I suspect that legalizing pot for a sustainable buzz is a very close second. And if puffing on this mysterious herb helps open up our minds a little bit to help us get through the great transformation that needs to take place, all the better.

7

Solar

THE HISTORY OF SOLAR ELECTRICITY, in many ways, sums up the hopes of this book by showing how an early dedication to getting things done, combined with a general disregard for observing convention, has led to the explosive growth and gradual acceptance of what was once considered a fringe energy source. Growing from humble backyard tinkering in its early days to a multi-billion dollar industry today, solar electricity has the capacity to one day knock planet-killing fossil fuels from their nefarious perch, and its early history exemplifies the "ask forgiveness rather than ask permission" approach to getting shit done that is so natural to me and dear to my heart. The early pioneers of solar electricity weren't so much breaking the law as they were just totally off the radar screen of any kind of government official. Much of this had to do with the fact that the revenue source for most of that early solar investment came from the subject of the last chapter — reefer. In a similar way to how pornography provided much of the initial revenue that later launched the rest of Internet commerce (one billion dollars in revenue and half of all Internet searches in 1998, for example), the pot-growing flower children up in the hills of Humboldt would take chunks of their clandestine profits and pay the then exorbitant price for a solar electric panel or two and some batteries. It was pretty much the only way to have some lights at night up in the deeply rural mountains, and fit in with the hippie self-sufficiency ethic that still prevailed in Northern California in the late 1970s and early '80s. The solar revolution was budding (*sorry!*).

I had a long chat with David Katz, a highly respected solar guru from the earliest days there, at his home in Arcata, California, and he gave me the skinny. David got started in solar back in 1979, after he bought some land in Humboldt county and built a home. At first he would charge up extra car batteries when he drove into town. When he returned home, he would plug his house into his car and run some lights and a stereo from the charged batteries. In 1980 he attended the Consumer Electronics Show in Las Vegas and a guy in one of the booths had some solar toys. David got the man to sell him a hundred solar panels and took them back to Humboldt, where he sold the lot in a few days. You didn't need to drive into town to have lights and music anymore. Alternative Energy Engineering was born, and David has worked in the business ever since.

All of these early systems were off the grid, meaning they only served the individual residence to which they were connected, and extra electricity was stored in car, and later marine, batteries. The money to buy these panels came almost exclusively from professional pot growers, who cherished their privacy up in the hills as much as their Rolling Stones records and being able to see after dark. Business was steady as the Emerald Triangle became an established weed growing area and many of the new residences wanted off-grid solar to power their homes.

The next stage of the solar electricity revolution was powered by fear rather than from a desire for San Franciscans to get stoned. The nineties were coming to a close, and with it, Western civilization itself. Y2K was going to wipe out all telecommunications, electricity generation and the ability of corn to grow or cows to produce milk. Silicon Valley was quivering in its loafers, and well-paid computer types started dumping tons of money into electricity for their compounds to save their families from the coming catastrophe. How would they survive without refrigeration and air conditioning? Solar electric (aka photovoltaic, or PV) systems got substantially bigger and more complex, and the increased interest and money started to bring improved products onto the scene, not just more efficient PV modules but also inverters, racking and other infrastructure. But another big thing happened. Some of these PV systems weren't just off-grid, they were backup systems to residences already tied to the grid, and the potential existed to tie them into the grid ("grid-tie") and pump solar electrons out into the world at large.

The first day of the new millennium arrived, and everything hummed along just as it had the day before. So Y2K was either the biggest scam ever perpetuated or a narrowly averted disaster that would have ruined industrial civilization save for the brilliant hard work of thousands of computer programmers. Maybe history will sort it out, although I've often found official history to be lacking in the truth department. At any rate, I can just barely figure out how to open up the Internet on my computer after I've had two cups of coffee, so I won't be the one to tell you anything about the history of computer programming. But here were all these backup PV systems, waiting to be tied to the grid. Solar electricity was entering the mainstream.

When our cob house was finished and my former wife and I started seriously looking into solar electricity in 2004, it was still in the waning days of do-it-yourself off-grid, at least in North Carolina. The grid-tied revolution was marching westward through the Southwest, but us bumpkins in North Carolina had no clue. We were just starting to cobble together the pieces for our small 310-watt off-grid system when Mr. Inspector showed up and asked what exactly in the hell we thought we were doing, building a house out of mud. As if that wasn't weird enough, we wanted to make our electricity from the sun? We had some "splaining to do," as they say in these parts.

God, fate, karma or the Cosmic Waiter, or whatever name you assign to the mysterious, gave us a reasonable and, even more amazing, *curious* inspector. Now that I've got almost another decade or so of dealing with inspectors behind me, I realize that finding one with this particular trait is like finding a restaurant at the beach that knows how to cook seafood without frying it. And at least in North Carolina, that is rare indeed. By this time we were learning more about the whole grid-tied phenomenon, and this actually elicited an interesting philosophical conundrum. Do you adopt the attitude of saying "Screw it," and keep all the sustainable juice for yourself, or do you take the first step in trying to get things rolling in a positive direction by sharing it with your energy-guzzling neighbors? Ultimately, this proved to be a moot point for us at this juncture, firstly because our PV array was miniscule to the point of hilarity, and secondly because our inspector, a trained electrician, made never tying to the grid a condition for approving our solar project. The question simmered though, and ultimately came down to whether you act out of fear or out of hope, and the potential ramifications of both. Or, phrased philosophically, do you pursue the perception of security or the evanescence of liberty?

My first solar stop was in Paonia, Colorado, which along with nearby Carbondale form the home base for Solar Energy International. I had helped teach and work on the curriculum for their sustainable building program, and spent a few days catching up with old acquaintances and taking in the beautiful surroundings. The drive from Carbondale to Paonia has to be one of the most beautiful in the world, with huge snow-capped peaks towering above as I wound my way up over McClure Pass and into the valley, the North Fork of the Gunnison River guiding me down towards Paonia. Ironically, this is big coal country, and the small towns seem rough and tumble. Huge silos of coal fill trains hundreds of cars long, which barrel down the valley a dozen or more times each day.

By contrast Paonia is a beacon of sustainability amongst the fossils. Students come from all over North America to study at SEI's state-of-the-art lab yard, and the rich alluvial soil and the water of the Gunnison help create vibrant commercial orchards, many of them organic, and many specializing in cherries. Showing up around cherry festival time on the Fourth of July is almost sure to result in a case of the runs, as it's almost impossible to stop eating those delicious fruits picked fresh from the tree. For a town of only about 3,000 folks, there's a lot of nightlife, much of it centered around drinking delicious concoctions from the local brewery, based out of a former church right in the center of town. In Paonia at least, Dionysus has won the battle of the gods.

I was there to spend some time with Ed Eaton, an acquaintance I'd met a few times before who I knew had been involved in solar electricity and solar cooking for several decades. He lives about 15 miles outside of Paonia near the town of Crawford, near a gravel road that leads to the Black Canyon National Park. Ed has made a habit out of living in converted school buses or other mobile vehicles for most of his adult life, and his current set up was enviable. His bus was parked in front of one of the most substantial cob homes I've ever encountered, one that Ed had helped the owners of the property build a few years back. A beautiful vegetable garden, complete with a flock of chickens, was framed by a panoramic view of the mountains of southwestern Colorado. Ed had his own garden in a small fenced-in enclosure around his bus, but it just had towering pot plants instead of anything nutritious. I must say that Ed makes some of the finest

Ed Eaton steps out of his solar bus nestled among the southwest Colorado Rockies to talk about his long involvement with all things solar.

pot cookies I've ever experienced, not only because he bakes them in his solar oven, but also because he makes them mild enough so you can remain relatively functional. When I arrived at around nine in the morning, the sun just peeking over the mountain, he made sure to hand me one as he tossed another in his mouth.

We sat for a good hour and a half, enjoying the morning sun on our faces, as Ed regaled me with his solar tales. One of the things I like most about Ed is his love of solar cooking, an enthusiasm I share. The world has gone nuts over solar electricity, a technology that typically captures around 15 percent of the sun's energy, while more basic technologies like solar hot water and solar cooking often have efficiencies around 60 percent, or four times as much. But Ed got his start in solar with cooking. While living in Tucson in 1980 Ed and his then-wife checked out a book on solar cooking from the library and were instantly smitten with the idea. They built their first oven out of recycled materials and some insulation they scavenged from a discarded fridge, spending about $16. The oven lasted for many years.

Then in 1982 they attended a solar cooking event in Scottsdale. They saw a wide array of cookers, and that was inspiring, but bummer of bummers, you couldn't try the food! So they decided right there to put on a solar cooking event in Tucson where you could.

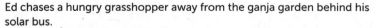

Ed chases a hungry grasshopper away from the ganja garden behind his solar bus.

The following year, with help from many friends, they staged the first annual Tucson Solar Potluck Exhibition. In 2011 the event was in its 29th year, the second longest continuous solar event in the US. The success of the Exhibition just got the pair that much more juiced, so they started experimenting with solar oven plans and selling them out of the classifieds of *Mother Earth News*. For three and a half years they lived in a converted school bus with their two daughters, cooking better than 90 percent of their meals with the sun. Later, in 1983, they established the still active non-profit Citizens for Solar to focus on public demonstrations of solar cooking at fairs and in parks, feeding locals and sometimes the homeless who were living on the streets. Ed got involved in solar electricity a few years later, working for Photocomm, an early distributor of photovoltaics based out of Scottsdale, Arizona. This was fascinating work too, but Ed had hatched an idea early in his solar career that he was determined to try once he got the opportunity: The Solar Cafe.

After working at Photocomm, Ed made the move to Carbondale to teach for SEI. In 1998, he was teaching the bulk of their photovoltaic workshops along with solar cooking and water pumping classes, and doing a fair amount of the day-to-day office stuff. As summer approached he realized he was getting burned out and wanted to be outside in the sun rather than just talking about it in the classroom. He reduced his hours and in May of that year set up his RV and a bunch of solar cookers in the parking lot of the Carbondale Council for the Arts on Tuesdays and Wednesdays. He didn't have any intention of making money but hoped to break even, and he used only organic vegetarian food sourced as locally as possible. His hope was that being on private property would keep him out of the purview of the authorities, and his confidence in this idea extended to allowing customers to drink beer or purchase a rum smoothie from his operation. His intention was to operate the cafe just during the summer, and only if it was a success. Which it was. Upwards of 50 customers a day came to eat lunch, which isn't surprising since Ed was working for free and paying no rent or utility bills, so the burritos and other goodies were often selling for just two or three dollars. Enthusiasts came from as far away as Aspen, 60 miles away, just to see the only known clandestine solar cafe in operation at the time.

Not surprisingly, in a small town like Carbondale, the shiny outdoor cafe on Main Street quickly caught the attention of the local authorities. At first they just wanted him to get a business license. Okay, no problem. But then the media got captivated by the story, and The Solar Cafe started showing up in the local rag and then on the local TV news and then an interview on Colorado Public Radio. Of course Ed the advocate ate up all the attention — that was the whole point! To get folks to contemplate the glory of the sun and how it can power our lives. But this brought with it the scrutiny of local officials. The last straw was a complaint from a local merchant, probably fearful of the cheap competition. The health inspector showed up. Things that were required were obviously missing, like permits and bleach. Ed was taken aback by this last item. "Bleach? Why would I

Here Ed explains the inner workings of his newest LED light, in front of the compound's composting toilet.

Cooking some falafel balls with a parabolic solar cooker at Solar Energy International in Paonia, Colorado.

have a poison near my organic foods?" And there was a dog in the RV where he was prepping food. Otherwise, it was spotless. The kitchen wasn't up to code, and, of course, it couldn't be, not just because it was almost entirely outside but also because there's no such thing as a code-compliant commercial solar oven for use in restaurants. The end result: a $2,000 a day fine for continuing to operate. With revenue in the $100 to $200 range, this was the death knell. Ed hasn't given up on the solar cafe idea, though, and he's still scheming on how to resurrect it, perhaps in Paonia rather than Carbondale. For now he's still baking his delicious vegetarian fare and pot cookies just outside his solar bus, bringing the goods to SEI potlucks and wherever else hungry people gather.

The previous summer I had also been out in Paonia, and along with Matt, another solar cooking aficionado and SEI'er, had busted out the parabolic solar cooker to fry some falafel balls one sunny evening. I'd never had the chance to use one of these puppies, and they are amazing. This one was about five feet wide and had a little rack in the middle to hold whatever you're cooking. My favorite part is how to tell if you have the solar cooker aimed correctly. All you do is line up the shadow of a small round bolt head sticking out of the side with an inscribed circle on the oven. A slight adjustment about every five minutes or so keeps the concentrated parabolized solar rays focused on your cookery. We were frying food using just the sun at 7:30 in the evening! And it was totally delicious. This time around we made another falafel frying date, but even in sunny Colorado the weather doesn't always cooperate, and the clouds forced us into the kitchen to use boring old fossil fuels to cook our food. Paonia is a special little place, a hidden Shangri-La tucked into the towering Rocky Mountains, and I ended up leaving a piece of my heart in that tiny burg. As my week there wrapped up, we had one last get together planned.

Folks in this part of Colorado are really into their pot and other drugs when available (which they were), and staying sober requires constant vigilance, like how you have to pay lots of attention at the dog park lest you soil your boots. Unfortunately, at the end of the week after a fabulous dinner of local goodies with old friends, sitting outside under the stars sipping fancy tequila, the Perseid meteor shower on full display in the clear cool night, I let my guard down. That last night in Paonia ended up being a wild one, perhaps one for the history books. Without getting into the sordid details, suffice it to say that as I left town the next morning with just an hour or so of sleep and headed through back country roads into Utah for a few days at Arches National Park, I felt as though I'd morphed into the Hunter S.

Recovering in Arches National Park after a very long night of revelry and more in Paonia the night before.

Thompson of sustainability writing, for whatever kind of sense that makes. Fortunately, a few mellow days looking at those amazing wonders allowed me to defrazzle my brain enough to allow me to journey westward, towards the hills of Humboldt…but I've already told you that story. My next visit to a solar guru didn't happen until I was way further up the West Coast.

One of the last stops on my big tour was to visit Ian Woofenden on Guemes Island, in Padilla Bay off the coast of Washington. Taking the ferry from Anacortes, I gave the 13-year-old Saturn a loving pat on the dash. I was a very, very long way from home, and crossing the channel to Guemes seemed to drive this point home emphatically. The car had 180,000 miles on it already, and giant mountains lurked all around, some of which would have to be partially scaled in order to begin the journey eastward.

Ian is an intense and amazing man. As one of the senior editors of *Homepower* magazine, author of *Wind Power for Dummies*, and long-time instructor for Solar Energy International, Ian has been fundamental in jump starting the revitalized wave of renewable electricity over the past two decades. At least equally amazing is how his love of renewable energy and three decades on Guemes have transformed the island into what must be one of the highest per capita residential installations of solar and wind in the US, if not the world. I had one day to see the island, and Ian planned out every minute of it. I'm not sure if we saw every single PV and wind installation on the island, but we must have come close. I showed up at around 9 AM, checking out the amazing homestead that Ian and his family of seven children have built up over the years. There was enough time to see the rambling barn-style house with a variety of vintage solar equipment in various states of operational condition, and to relieve myself in the largest composting toilet I've ever seen in my life. It was two stories tall and had separate chambers for alternating years, and a clever flag operated by a pulley to let everyone know when it's occupied. I guess with nine family members you can turn out some serious humanure! But I didn't have long to contemplate this goliath. Ian had the tires on the bikes pumped up and was raring to go.

Ian is very libertarian in his outlook, and despite being a solar and wind genius knows almost nothing (or at least pretends to) about codes, the legality of what's being done, what the inspector has to say or any of that. Not that the little island of Guemes is lawless, but it shares a sheriff with the mainland, and he doesn't seem to bother to come over unless there's something pressing. And from the folks I met there, that's just fine with them. In fact, it's one of the reasons they live there. Things have changed in Ian's time, however, and not to his liking. The building inspector was much more of a presence on the island of late, and Ian's freewheeling homestead would likely not pass muster if he tried to build it today.

I won't be as thorough as Ian in describing all the places we visited. For the most part, they were fairly typical PV installations, but there was a very impressive wind installation at a construction site up on

Dave and Janet's outdoor solar shower on the edge of their giant vegetable garden. Keeping it simple, but making it beautiful.

the mountain. Our host explained that he had been building their home for almost 15 years, what with planning, scrapping ideas and false starts. Meanwhile his desire for a wind turbine became overpowering, so he turned his attention to that and he and Ian busted it out. Then he put a big PV array *on* the wind tower, which seemed like a great idea. Now he had a bunch of renewable juice — but no house! Ian seemed to appreciate the man's priorities, but most folks would have done it in the reverse order.

Two spots we visited definitely piqued my interest. The first was a little homestead tucked into the deep woods of the island, not too far from the ferry terminal. Lots of folks building their own home aim for some level of self-sufficiency, but few ultimately come very close to achieving this ideal. This couple, who I'll call Dave and Janet, had come about as close as anyone I've ever come across. A very cute 400 square foot cabin, built of locally-milled wood and salvaged windows and other materials sat catty-corner to another smaller studio building, donated by some acquaintances who no longer wanted it. This additional building was a source of consternation for Dave and Janet, who had felt they had enough space in the small cabin they'd built, but hadn't been able to resist accepting the smaller studio space. It also added to their strained relationship with the building inspector, who had eventually discovered the couple back in the woods and raised Cain about the lack of permits, so now the project sat in a state of legal limbo, their residence unsanctioned by the authorities. It was very hard to see what harm would come from leaving this couple alone. They collected their own rainwater, composted their own humanure, grew much of their food in a sprawling two-acre garden, took solar heated showers out in the sun and powered their fridge and lights with a small PV system. They seemed perfectly content to just spend their time existing and being. The couple, probably in their forties, had made the choice to be child-free and live close to the earth in an integrated and simple way. Yet their existence was illegal. You can't compost your crap. You need to have indoor plumbing and a separate room for your bathroom. Your windows need to be double-pane and NFRC-certified...et cetera, et cetera. Opting out of the system is not an option, even if you do it on a small island in the middle of nowhere in the most ecologically sensitive way possible.

It was sad to hop on our bikes and leave this little Walden and pedal to our next destination, but Ian had a self-imposed schedule to keep, and there was plenty more to see. The very next spot had the same theme of self-sufficiency but was so different in its application that it threw my mind for a jolt. Ian gave me a few words of introduction to each of the spots we visited, but mostly he just let me discover each one on my own by asking questions of the owners, or him if they were absent. Later on, while we were biking to the next destination, he would fill in more details. So all I knew when I pedaled up to this particular spot was that it was "George's Place," which, of course, meant nothing to me. What was perhaps the most impressive thing about my day on Guemes was that Ian had arranged not just for us to visit over a dozen spots on the island, but he'd also arranged to have the owners present to give a personal tour of each property most times. And this was on a Thursday when you might have thought everyone would be busy working! Only later in the evening would I discover that he was busy the next day, leaving to Puerto Rico for two weeks to teach a solar class. Instead of preparing for his journey, he'd had to arrange this massive solar tour of the island. But all that just seemed to make him more energetic and get more done. Ian was the perfect embodiment of the adage that if you want to get something done, you give it to the busy person, not the one sitting around on their butt.

We coasted down the driveway into an opening that contained an RV and three white steel shipping containers, one smallish and two large, with plenty of solar equipment perched on top. On the edge of the woods in front of another red storage container, George was puttering around in a grassy opening, dressed in white pants, white shirt and a white hat. He was messing with some PV modules on racks mounted on wheels for easy portability. Portability was an idea that George cultivated, partly due to a peripatetic inclination, but mostly because maintaining an aura of portability kept the building inspector from hassling him. Basically, George used the three white storage containers as large rooms in an outdoor living space. None of them had windows, of course, but who needs windows when you spend most of the daylight hours outdoors during the summer, and the winters are so dark and dreary you don't want to look outside anyways?

The smaller white shipping container had an evacuated tube solar hot water heater mounted on top. The inside was impeccably clean and organized, and functioned as George's solar laundry. At the entrance, a few white clothing items were suspended from a solar clothes dryer (aka a clothesline). A red warning light was programmed to go off when the tank full of water was all heated, setting the stage for a full afternoon of clothes washing. The solar laundry's smaller size meant George could take it to a campsite or festival, although it wasn't clear if this ever happened, or if George just used it to keep his clothes really, really white.

We toured the other two large shipping containers, which acted as the residence proper, with a kitchen and a bed and a couch for lounging. The southernmost shipping container had a large PV array mounted on top. Both of these containers were filled with lots of gadgets, all of them, of course, powered by the sun. It didn't take me long to realize that George was a kind of solar electrical savant, and things like motors and pumps and volts made complete sense to him

Dave and Janet's small hand-built cabin exemplifies their simple and romantic life. Unfortunately, the inspector was not impressed.

George's solar laundry, built in a portable steel storage container. The red light flashes when the water is hot enough to start washing.

in a way that my brain would never be able to process or fully comprehend. He and Ian had some long convoluted conversations about things like batteries and meters, and I tried to pay attention and take notes, but often found myself staring off into the nearby woods daydreaming about squirrels. The whole compound was utilitarian in the extreme, in such a way that it embodied its own minimalist aesthetic. George had managed to build a mostly self-sufficient abode (the garden was noticeably absent) out of pre-manufactured parts for a very reasonable amount of money, without actually having to build anything himself, not something he was terribly interested in anyways. It's always amazing to see an example of something you've attempted to achieve yourself but would never in a million years have come at in this exact way. I was deeply impressed with George's accomplishments even if I had a little difficulty understanding his aesthetic.

At this point we hadn't even eaten lunch, and our whirlwind tour of solar Guemes was just gaining steam. We traded in our bikes for my car and started to scope some of the more far flung spots, seeing some great gems like the aforementioned homeless wind tower, a solar roof embedded in metal panels and a geothermally heated new home with a green roof and a fantastic view of the bay. By five o'clock I was pretty much dying for a cold beer from all the talking and biking and poking around up on sunny roofs. We made it back to Ian's homestead, where one of his sons and a friend were taking turns plunging into a muddy pond on a giant rope swing suspended high in the air from a cable strapped 40 or 50 feet up between two Douglas firs, the kind of killer rope swing you can make when your specialty is building wind towers. It looked terrifying but the call was irresistible. I took a half-dozen or so swings, almost peeing in my shorts each time as I flew through the air and let go high above the little swimming hole. The water was cold, but a warm outdoor solar shower awaited. This would have been enough of a day as it was, and I was ready to cook some food, set up camp and crawl into my sack, but Ian convinced me to head over to some friends' house in what he described as a "strawbale yurt" (how was I going to turn that down?) and play some music. We biked another five miles and jammed for a while. On the way there Ian revealed that he was leaving for Puerto Rico to teach the next day, and he was going to ride his bike to the airport. I tried to think where there might be a nearby airport, remembering my drive up the day before from Seattle, about one hundred miles to the south.

"What airport?" I asked, although I was pretty sure I already knew the answer.

"Seattle," he replied. My legs ached that much more just from thinking about it, but it did somehow make my own journey back eastward seem less onerous.

Interview with Ed Eaton

Q: The solar bus you live in is very cool. You have a long history of living in this "semi-nomadic" way. Explain how this relates to your view of how we should live upon the earth, and how this looser idea of what we would call "home" has affected your views on living sustainably.

A: First I must say that home is where the heart lies. That could be in a nice house, apartment, garage, rec vehicle, teepee, tent, car, boat, truck, school bus or just out under the stars. I have done all the above.

In school buses, three times. Others who have not been as fortunate as me live in box cars, storm drains, under bridges, in refugee camps and worse.

I feel very fortunate to have been born here in the good old US. But most of us have no idea what it is like to live outside of the comforts of a modern home. Most of us have no idea what goes in to providing power and other utility services to our homes. We just flip the switches to turn up the heat, reach for the remote, flush the toilet, pay the rent, pay the mortgage, live by the rules, spread out and end up owning more than we need. All this while living in McMansion-style structures with lots of room for ourselves and all the shit we own. Most of us seem married to our leases and mortgages and unable to break free from the bond of debt.

I have struggled with the concept of going into debt to let the bank own my home. I choose to have the ability to move from one spot to another. Have as small an impact on Mother Earth as possible. It is my belief that we need to be more responsible, on a personal level, for the energy we use, the waste we create, the pollution we produce, the footprint we plant, the area we take up and the others that we impact.

I ask myself if it is possible to be sustainable without taking personal responsibility. Living in a small habitat like a bus, teepee or modest-size house off the grid has some distinct advantages. One can get a better handle on their energy needs and so forth. For example, when you have to take care of your own trash you become much more cognizant of how much you are really creating. You begin to manage things differently. You are the one doing the work. When you are relying on sunshine to cook or charge your batteries you pay more attention to your energy use patterns. When you compost your human waste you pay more attention. You take it outside yourself, not flush it with water somewhere else.

Sustainability? Sustenance farmers are the ones living sustainably. All the rest of us are striving for it. If you think about it over the eons all peoples have had many, many challenges surviving and living here on planet Earth.

Most were not experiencing the thought of, "Are we fucking the planet up for future generations?" They were not polluting the sky, filling up landfills with trash, depleting the natural resources, etc. Their challenges were different yet similar to one who lives without the excesses of the modern human today.

They were personally responsible for their heat, food, dealing with their own waste, raising crops and animals, figuring out how to take a warm bath. Taking responsibility for your own shit. That's what sustainability means to me. Whether it is in a home, a bus or whatever.

Yet we are faced with disdain when we try to live more freely. Even more so, sustainably. There are rules and zoning and compliance issues. "Sorry Ed you can only live on this property for 90 days in a non-permanent structure." "But it is 25 acres basically in the middle of nowhere out here in the sticks!" "Does not matter. Rules are rules." "By the way, what do you do with, well you know, your poop?" "I compost it." "No shit?" "No shit man."

In Boulder, Colorado it is against the law to be homeless. Not strictly enforced but against the law.

Q: Many folks today hear "solar" and think solar electricity. You're a seasoned expert in solar electricity, but you also have a broader and more inclusive view of how solar can be used, especially for cooking. Based on this experience, what do you see as the best means for individuals to become engaged with solar energy. How should it be integrated into our lives and society?

A: First one has to realize that the passive attributes of the Sun far outweigh the active methods. Solar thermal applications are much more efficient than photovoltaics. All passive applications contribute to energy efficiency and energy efficacy.

The best modern example I can think of is the electric clothes dryer. How wasteful. What is the efficiency of a clothesline either outdoors or indoors? I have a friend who replaced the AC motor in one with a more efficient DC motor and removed the heating element. He built a 4 foot by 10 foot hot air collector and with a very small muffin fan directed the heated air into the clothes dryer. The DC motor turned the tumbler directly from his battery supply. When not using the dryer the heated air was directly ducted into the living space during the winter months.

The bigger question is how was solar energy removed from our everyday lives? Passive solar energy is not rocket science. It is what I refer to as "caveman technology." A simpler observation of the past will support the greater use of Sun energy for today. Our grandparents have a better understanding than our youth. They all had clothes lines.

There are many areas that must be addressed including education, legislation, demonstration and implementation. I have always been in favor of solar cooking as an instrument of education. We all have to eat. It is a common bond that all folks enjoy. Look where it drove me.

Q: What needs to change about the law in order for solar to become more widespread?

A: In my opinion it is not about laws. It is about breaking the mold of doing business as usual. Nobody made any rules or laws that say we must burn coal or drive all over the place or fly away on vacations or waste water or flush shit down the drain. These facilities were created by entrepreneurs who saw good business opportunities by making our lives easier.

It seems that more and more people are identifying with the externalities associated with our easier modern way of life. The goal is to look forward for better solutions both technical and practical. Einstein wrote that insight is *more* important than expertise. I say going backwards sometimes is going forwards. Down with the clothes dryer and up with the clothes line. Focus on practical solutions and give the engineers some time off.

We all already live in a solar powered world. We need to celebrate the Sun as the giver of all life as we know it. Break away from our nostalgic lifestyles and begin to think forward by forgetting about coal, oil and natural gas, Ronald Reagan, Western movies and gas guzzling cars. Shut down the nuke plants and make our move. Begin the transition to a renewable energy society focusing on low impact lifestyles and solutions. We did not break out of the Stone Age because we ran out of rocks.

8

Green Anarchism

NOTHING WENT MORE to the core of the question, "What is sustainable?" than my visit to Wildroots, a small cadre of "neoprimitivists" tucked into the southern Appalachian mountains, and a green anarchist rendezvous outside of Asheville. Since being a teenager in the early '90s I had been interested in anarchism, at the time in a process of incorporating ecological principles and branching off into what is now generally called green anarchism. Growing up in suburban Raleigh, North Carolina, (actually the sprawling soulless security of nearby Cary) I had felt surrounded by an endless sterility, filled with shopping malls and video games meant to distract me and my fellow suburb-dwellers from our empty existence.

I picked up copies of *Anarchy: A Journal of Desire Armed* from the used book store, Reader's Corner, stole copies of Proudhon and Emma Goldman from the North Carolina State library, and posted mimeographed flyers declaring revolution on Hillsborough St., heavily under the influence of dextromethorphan hydrobomide (cough syrup) and the lingering effects of a very psychedelic high school experience. A friend and I had stolen the mimeograph machine from a nearby elementary school. I thought I knew everything but actually knew almost nothing, except for a core feeling that the way of the world was wrong.

The year after high school was marked by a deep restlessness, part of which manifested itself in a desire to ride my bicycle across the country. I trained (some) with a friend who wanted to come along, but gave up the idea once crunch time came. I borrowed my brother's ten-speed and bought a ticket from Raleigh to Portland for $80 on the gray dog. I had a friend, Eugene, going to Reed college there, and it seemed like as good a place on the West Coast as any to start. There was no room in his small dorm, and I was trying to pull off the entire trip for $300, so a hotel was obviously out of the question. In those pre-Internet days, there was a group called the Crash Network where folks offered up their homes for fellow travelers to stay. For a week I ended up at the home of Feral Faun, one of the leading writers synthesizing anarchist thought with a desire for rewilding the human spirit in tune with nature. At his home I was introduced to his writings, which can to some degree be summed up by his words: "I want to know the free-spirited wildness of my unrepressed desires realizing themselves in festive play. I want to smash down every wall that stands between me and the intense, passionate life of untamed freedom that I want. The sum of these walls is everything we call civilization, everything that comes between us and the direct participatory experience of the wild world."

Green anarchism held my thoughts for a while, but was eventually overpowered by my engineering nature — I wanted to build something, do something, use my hands to solve problems. Although I love to hang out in the woods, I quickly find myself overcome with the desire to create, mold, alter, for what I hope is the greater good. Does this make me part of the problem? I'm not sure. There's no doubt that the dynamics of our current society create a profound underlying instability in our lives, something that wouldn't occur if we lived in the equilibrium of a more "primitive" society, that gave us time to enjoy the day with playfulness, and provided a more solid foundation for what generally brings us the most happiness — our relationships with others and nature. But in a world that seemed to have condemned itself to disaster by its indifference and laziness, its gluttony and thrill-seeking, I couldn't come to terms with the idea of hanging out in the woods "playing," as Feral Faun had put it. I had to "do."

Two decades later in July 2010, I found myself driving up to the neoprimitivist Firefly Gathering in the mountains of southwest North Carolina. After two decades of fermenting, green anarchy had become palpably alive. Seeing the several hundred people gathered amongst the old log cabins and recreational lake of a mountain retreat, many dressed in deer hides, some carrying bundles of thatch and sticks for making baskets or impromptu rafts, I realized it had become a bona fide movement.

I have never been a big fan of cars — at times I truly detest them and try to swear off them forever like a smoker often does at the end of each pack — but their utility, given our current infrastructure, prohibits such noble sentiments from becoming reality. Winding up the roads in my old Saturn wagon to the "rendezvous," as the gathering was referred to by its participants, I was very curious about how everyone else got there. There were plenty of cars in the parking lot, and just like looking through someone's mail, you can tell a lot about any gathering of people by spending a few minutes in the parking lot. There was certainly a fair percentage of biofueled diesels, along with a wide spectrum of pickup trucks, from the ancient to the sparklingly new. There were several high-end vehicles, including a Mercedes SLK 380 — probably an $80,000 car that I ended up parked next to. It was hard for my mind to reconcile this pristine luxury vehicle with the fresh fly-covered deer skin staked out on the tennis court nearby.

A deer hide waiting to be tanned, one of the traditional or "primitive" skills being taught at the Firefly Gathering in the mountains of North Carolina.

Except for the luxury vehicles, almost all had a few bumper stickers, proclaiming everything from their love of roadkill opossum to the imminence of industrial society's collapse. My own car's bumper stickers advertising my local food co-op and my love of renewable energy appeared naïvely hopeful.

After check-in, my first whirl through the menagerie lived up to expectations. I didn't feel like I'd gone back in time — there were too many relics of consumerist society to create that mirage — but things were different enough to provide that pleasant sensation of new experience, that cracking open of the mind and the brain-jostling that accompanies the unique and the spectacular. Ascending the hill towards the canteen, naked children proliferated, with one young boy of eight or so sporting such natty dreadlocks as to make any Rastafarian nod in approval. Two young men in front of the canteen, their hair and beards a nightmare for any barber, played fiddles with modest skill, grins on their faces, their nakedness a declaration of freedom as cogent as Jefferson's famous manifesto.

The July day was warm, with peals of thunder and splatterings of occasional large raindrops falling threateningly. It was the gathering's third day of four and the atmosphere was ripe. Bathing, except for a skinny dip in the lake, seemed frowned on, wet wood smoke hung in the air, and the humidity brought out the rich fetid smell of hides drying in the occasional sun in preparation for a "brain tan." The gatherings, I was to learn, often break down into two camps: the dilettantes, and the more hardcore primitivists who attempt to live within the strict bounds of their anti-technology fervor. The hardcore group included many of the skills teachers, their classes covering a wide range from fire making and trapping to blowguns and basketry. From talking with frequent participants, there's an undeniable competitiveness within the hardcore group, much of it revolving around the eating of roadkill. Rumor has it that at the fall rendezvous later that year a roadkill puppy was butchered and cooked over an open fire for one of the dinners. I am a person who hates waste, but I am still having trouble "digesting" this piece of news. Undoubtedly, I shared with everyone present at the gathering a deep love of nature, and the existence of physical waste — i.e., trash — can be considered an embodiment of our disregard and disconnection from the natural world. Certainly eating roadkill puppy eliminates some of this waste, but I also expect a level of beauty from our daily interaction with nature. I was having trouble reconciling these competing sentiments as I pictured a young pooch turning on a spit, but perhaps this is only because I still have to overcome some (or much) of my lingering cultural prudishness that seeks to ban all images of death and dismemberment from our collective brain, especially as it relates to our meat-engorging American cuisine.

On the second day I felt an unusual calm come over me. Partly, this was just relief at actually having left on my big road trip, with all the petty tasks of travel preparation behind me. After much random meandering through the gathering, I also realized another source of the calm. Of all the clothes that people wore — the deer skins of the more hardcore, the rugged flannels of the sprinkling of mountain folk, the modest clothing of the students, and of course the nakedness — almost none of it contained writing or ads of any type. In contrast to the plethora of bumper stickers on the vehicles in the parking lot, no one seemed to be advertising any ideas, products, colleges, groups or anything else on their clothing. It was just a beautiful day, surrounded by interesting people deep in the mountains and without any commercial interruptions. My thoughts were their own, no one was trying to hijack them for their own agenda. Stripped of this constant nagging, so prevalent elsewhere, I found myself operating with a fundamentally improved attitude towards my fellow participants. I went to the trouble of changing into a wordless shirt so as to not violate their own sense of relief from information bombardment. So many of us, present company included, proclaim parts of their identity on their clothing. To some extent, of course, this was true here as well, but it was subtle, and consisted more of what the clothing was made of rather than overwhelming passersby with words and images.

Perhaps the best description of the event would be "a punk Boy Scout camping trip." There was definitely a pervading earnestness. People made distraught by their truncated relationship with nature and lack of self-sufficiency were learning to function out in the wilds on a fundamental level. I took a class on trapping from Colbert, a seasoned raconteur who had dropped out of his lucrative career in finance to live, trap and just be in the swamps of south Georgia. I was delighted to discover that an activity I had never thought about for more than two seconds in my life turned out to be almost infinitely complex, and as a hobby provides an almost unparalleled means for studying the intricacies of nature. Colbert approached trapping with a beguiling distaste for work — why sit for hours in the woods hunting when you could use your wits to trap. Tom Sawyer would certainly approve. Primitive trapping is all about understanding animal behavior, and using materials readily at hand to catch game. Often the game is still alive after you trap it. The best way to dispatch a trapped animal, apparently, is to club it on the back of the neck. Up until this point I was getting very excited about my new trapping hobby. I've raised poultry and dispatched quite a few. I'm a big believer in meat-eaters like myself at least occasionally killing the food they eat. I had to ask myself, am I really too much of a wimp to kill an animal by clubbing it on the back of the head? My guess is, once you set a trap and catch one, there's not much choice but to go ahead and steel yourself and get it over with. Since many trapped animals will attack you if you try to set them free, there would be little choice, but I'm going on speculation here.

The Saturday night bonfire started off with some fine storytelling by a few of the movement's elders, telling of their epiphanies about the wonders of nature through chance encounters like accidentally catching a pair of mountain trout using just their bare hands. As darkness crept over the gathering and the sparks shot up into the night, the mixed gathering of hardcore anarchists and dreadlocked trustifarians on a weekend jaunt from Asheville all broke out their drums and starting banging. I was trying to keep my mind open in a writerly capacity, but the exhaustion from leaving on my trip overwhelmed me and I found myself hiding in my tent sucking on a warm can of Pabst and tucking myself in for the night before things really got going. I heard the shrieks of wild hippies calling out through the dense woods as I dozed off into my night's slumber.

Ultimately, as the gathering wound down the next day, and although there was a good deal of positive energy from the event, I was happy to hit the road. Part of this was my interaction with one of the organizers of the event. Since I was staying an extra night, I volunteered to help clean up the last evening, only to be treated with contempt and rather severely chastised for being slow, mostly because I hadn't received proper instructions for my volunteer task. I understood that hosting such an event must be enormously stressful, but my undeserved tongue-lashing brought to the surface a criticism often made by those who view their involvement in primitivism more as a hobby. Many of the hardcore primitivists seem to have developed the attitude that the average citizen living out in the regular world is worthy only of contempt, and even hatred, for living lives that deplete our collective resources and bring on ecological catastrophes such as global climate disruption. This may be the inevitable result of a belief that only a small percentage of the world's current population could live as primitivists without crowding each other out. The reduction in population to a theoretically sustainable level will be caused by waves of disease, war and famine, and the belief in such a die-off is widespread and almost an article of faith. Many seem to look forward to it with relish. While such a massive die-off is certainly a possibility in the near future, and one that, at times, I have come to believe in, experience has allowed me the circumspection and humility to realize that the future is unwritten, and depends on how our society can evolve and respond to these crises over the next few decades. Taking a die-off for granted this early in the likely descent of our civilization is premature and, if such an attitude becomes widespread, even potentially self-reinforcing. While there was a genuine desire among the gathering's participants to repair a badly broken relationship between themselves and nature, there was no discernible motivation to reform the broader relationship between society at large and the natural world.

During my downtime at the event, I was also given great pause by reading *Absalom, Absalom* by William Faulkner. The philosophy of green anarchism has more holes in it than most major organized religions, and my enjoyment of *Absalom, Absalom* became a proxy for my love of all the fine arts. Considering what a society would look like if a neoprimitivist viewpoint came to fruition, I kept asking myself, "What about Faulkner?" I tried to imagine some *Fahrenheit 451* scenario where each individual had memorized one of the classics, but what of the other fine arts? Woven baskets are certainly beautiful, but what about the masterpieces? Would I be able to be happy without the musical wonders of Charles Mingus, Hank Williams and Pavement? What about Van Gogh and Kandinsky? Frank Lloyd Wright and Sun Ray Kelley? Kant and Charles Bukowski? One should love truth and beauty, and despise those who try to destroy it for their own ends. Nature is only one half of what creates and preserves these two values. The other is, of course, humanity. Ultimately, any philosophy or way of life that only has room for one or the other is going to hold my attention for only a little while.

I followed up my weekend at the Firefly Gathering with a visit to Wildroots, a neoprimitivist camp in the mountains of North Carolina, later that fall. I had met Tod Krenshaw briefly at the gathering and traded a few phone calls and e-mails (yes, e-mails). I drove up after lunch from Durham, thinking I could make it there in one afternoon. But it was about an hour deeper into the woods than I expected, and I had to shell out for a hotel room and make it there the next morning. I got up early. It was a beautiful autumn day, perhaps the most magical time to be in the southern Appalachians. The undulating mountains were bedazzled by fall color, looking like enormous vibrant pillows that a giant child would enjoy rolling around on.

It wasn't long until I was stuck in traffic with lots of other leaf-peepers. SUVs and RVs blocked my view. I was soon to discover that most of these recreational vehicles, representing temporary homes occupied a few weeks a year at most, were several times larger than the permanent residences at Wildroots. Most of the congestion was caused by road construction, the quaint two-lane road in the process of being expanded to four lanes. The feeling of charm dying was palpable in the autumn air, as the giant fossil fuel-powered dinosaurs used their enormous buckets to reshape mountains into injured piles of dirt. All this is necessary to bring in the buyers of second homes, baby boomers from Atlanta, Charlotte and Raleigh-Durham, carving up steep mountainsides into suburban tracts almost identical to where the buyers come from. The North Carolina Department of Transportation is notorious for its paving madness, perpetuating a never-ending building and widening of roads throughout the state, with no thought to climate change, peak oil or mass transit. They are an unstoppable juggernaut of unsustainability.

I finally found the entrance and lurched up until I got my rental car stuck at the crest of the drive. Wildroots is laid out around a mountain cove (or "hollow" as they're often referred to in those parts), and most of the buildings and activity are on an old logging road carved into the side of the hollow, making a *V* where the old road pivots at the center of the cove. I walked past a few small earthen structures, poking my nose into the library and what looked like a blacksmithing area, until I finally heard voices and saw smoke bubbling out a wattle and daub long house with poplar bark roofing. I called out and was invited in. A group of six sat around an open hearth, drinking tea and

Coming into Wildroots, a year-round neoprimitivist encampment in western North Carolina. Past Tod's ancient and seldom used diesel, Talia works on the edible forest garden in front of the wattle and daub library.

discussing the day's plans. After introductions, I was offered a bagel salvaged from a recent dumpster-diving expedition at the nearest little burg, which Talia, one of my hosts, then toasted over the open fire on a small metal grill and smeared with bear fat. It was quite tasty, and I wolfed it down.

Tod and Talia are a long-term couple and the primary residents of Wildroots. When I visited there was only one other full-time resident, who left for a few days soon after my arrival. They are in their mid-forties, very intelligent dropouts from mainstream society. Some readers may consider the way they live to be extreme to the point of madness, but let me assure all in advance that is not the case. They *are* possessed of a deep faith in the imminent collapse of industrial society, and a more fundamental belief that all technology is ultimately used more for destruction than good, and that advances in technology only tend to accelerate the destruction. This writer considers these philosophical positions to be as valid as the opposite and much more prevalent faith that technology will save us from all our woes.

Almost every time I brought up my visit to Wildroots with more mainstream folks I got allusions to the Unabomber, so now is as good a time as any in the narrative to bring up the specter of primitivist and anarchist revolutionary Ted Kaczynski. Kaczynski was heavily influenced by Jacques Ellul, a theologian and Christian anarchist, who was fascinated and terrified by the prospects of deep thought control resulting from our ever-increasing dependence upon technology, and the resulting decrease in our self-sufficiency and direct contact with nature. I was sincerely fascinated with Ted Kaczynski in my youth. His manifesto came out when I was 20, just starting college and still very much under the influence of anarchism and the writings of Feral Faun. After reading Kaczynski's manifesto, I was curious to read more. Parts of it seemed intuitively right, such as our disconnection from nature, but the aspects of the manifesto relating to "technique" were baffling. Ellul's concern was that living in a technological society is so fundamentally different from living in a "primitive" culture that our thought patterns become radically altered. Instead of society being organized around the maintenance and well-being of our tribe and the immediately surrounding ecology that provides our sustenance, we are turned into devouring machines. Every day we must increase, grow, extract more, consume, etc., not because we want to, but because our thought patterns have been restructured to do this without thinking. Destruction is now "natural" to us.

Was Kaczynski crazy? Yes, he was. He thought he could start a one-man revolution — probably as clear a criterion of insanity as any. Revolutions require, if not a majority of a society, at least a large minority to support them. Rather than use his vast intelligence (and passable writing skills) to lay out his case and start creating a base of support, he just started blowing up people at random. So why mention this crazy person at all?

It's always interesting to take things to extremes, if only to see the range of options and to consider where in the middle the answer lies. Kaczynski figured out that the world was screwed up. Beyond that, he achieved nothing substantive and caused much misery. He was much more of a homicidal crank than a primitivist, and I write about him with trepidation. But since he came up again and again, I wanted to disassociate anyone in this chapter from his legacy. Although many primitivists evince a dislike, or at best disregard, for the average citizen, they certainly do not actively want to kill anyone. With the specter of ecological ruin and peak oil now so nigh, perhaps they don't feel they would have to, even if they had any inclination to do so. Instead, the energy of this movement is concentrated on taking positive, active steps to learn forgotten skills, to teach and create community with fellow activists and to try and reintegrate themselves into nature. More than anything they are concerned citizens with an extremely well-developed sense of responsibility for the effects their personal actions have on the world surrounding them.

Talking with Tod and Talia during my visit, it was interesting to discover their low opinion of the utility of philosophy, at least at this point in their lives. Their decision had been made. It was enough now to focus on living, to acquiring new skills that would make their lives more self-sufficient. It was fall, and time for shoring up the firewood supply. I took turns with a few of the other visitors and interns with the two-man bucksaw, setting up logs on a pair of bucks fabricated from forked logs, and heaving back and forth until the section of firewood fell to the ground, always concerned lest it roll off the small section of relatively flat ground and tumble down the mountain into the rhododendrons. Wildroots had decided to forgo chain saws this year and try to cut all their wood by bucksaw. I admired this integrity, having always vowed that I would use my last ounce of gasoline in my chainsaw, given the tremendous amount of work it accomplished compared with moving a human being a few hundred yards down the road in a car. Here were folks trying to eliminate fossil fuels from even the most necessary of activities.

I had never used a two-man bucksaw before, and it was interesting to compare how easy it was with some folks, and difficult with others. There seemed to be a natural matching of rhythm between some, and I wondered if this went to some deeper natural affinity (or dis-affinity) between us. Cutting logs into firewood has always been a noisy and solitary activity, my ears plugged up and copious quantities of other protective gear isolating me not just from any potential danger but also removing me from my surrounding environment and the

Tod splits wood, cut into sections using a bucksaw, for the fire in the common house.

wood I'm cutting. Now I had to actively work with another person, and the rhythmic noise of pulling the blade across the log was hypnotizing. Why snoring is referred to as "sawing logs" was revealed to me for the first time. As the beautiful leaves from the hardwoods floated down around us — brilliant reds from the maples, purples from the sweet gums, yellows from the hickories — pileated woodpeckers hammered on snags and a caucus of crows discussed the upcoming winter.

After an hour or so of this, I switched to chopping the round logs into quarters with a maul and then into much smaller sections, almost kindling, with an ax. The idea was to generate very dry wood with lots of surface area, so that the open fire in the common house, vented by two openings at the top of either gable, would burn hot and relatively smoke free. I'm good at chopping wood, and this satisfying activity provided a welcome respite to worrying about some ongoing turmoil in my personal life. I spent a few hours at this, and then my stomach started to growl. Lunch is generally dispensed with at Wildroots, but I wasn't in a mood to fast through this meal. I headed to my rental car, finding the others sitting next to a tarp filled with Chinese chestnuts harvested from a neighbor's tree. After being cracked, the nuts are allowed to dry for a few days; the meat pulls away from the shell and is easily removed. This gave me some concrete knowledge. I had planted a few chinquapins, an understory tree closely related to the American chestnut but not as susceptible to blight, a couple of years back at my home in Durham and had just a week or so earlier harvested a large crop of these native nuts. Yet I had been unable to easily remove the nut meat from the shell. Now I knew how.

I had a bounty of store-bought goods, and everyone was happy to take a share of peanut butter sandwiches, boiled eggs, root beer and potato chips. Being conventionally-minded by comparison, I was glad to see everyone eating some "normal" food. I was conscious of how silly this attitude was, but couldn't ignore feeling like I was offering up a genuine meal compared with what to me would feel like a subsistence diet of things like salvaged bagels with bear fat. I would guess that the feeling was reciprocated during the meals I was served during my stay.

Tod and Talia's wattle and daub sleeping hut, roofed with poplar bark,
perched on the side of a beautiful hollow.

From talking socially as we all worked on the chestnuts after lunch,
and later that night at dinner, I began to realize my welcome would
perhaps not last long in this little hollow. First, there's the annoyance
of having a writer or journalist document and examine your every
move. I've personally experienced this on a couple of occasions, and
it has consistently made me realize that people like politicians and
actors, who can continuously tolerate this level of personal intrusion,
are basically askew. But on a more fundamental level I represented an
alternate viewpoint and range of responses to peak oil and the waning
of industrial society from the narrative of collapse that Tod and Talia
had been telling themselves. Although younger, my initiation to the
trauma of peak oil awareness had come several years before theirs. I
had passed through a several-year-long certainty that sudden collapse
was the only possibility. Finally, my brain had loosened enough to
accept other possibilities and realize that the future is unknowable.
Two nails in this ideological coffin were my misjudging the financial

collapse of 2008, which I assumed would result in anarchy, and two books by John Michael Greer, *The Long Descent* and *The Ecotechnic Future*, which I feel provide a convincing rationale for an alternative outcome. Greer writes with too much conviction in his viewpoint, which he terms "catabolic collapse," referring to a long, possibly several-hundred-year process of gradual reductions in societal complexity, generated by a prolonged series of crises in energy availability and ecological destruction, but his premise is sound and well reasoned.

Rather than run away into the woods, I had moved from the woods into the city. If we are going to make the transition to a sustainable society without a massive die-off and reduction to primitivist living, then retrofitting our existing infrastructure is of paramount importance. It was with this in mind that I had moved to downtown Durham with my then-wife, retrofitted the house we bought to eliminate the use of any fossil fuels, and wrote *The Carbon-Free Home* to show others the potential of using our existing infrastructure in a sustainable way. Many folks I've spoken with over the years that are worried about peak oil and ecological destruction have at some point evinced a desire to move out to the woods and go off-grid. At the risk of sounding catty, if you happen to meet me after having read this, please don't express this desire to me. I've gone down that path already, and realized the error of my ways. To my mind, in most cases it is personal fear, and probably little else, that motivates us to think like this. I know because I've succumbed to it myself. Deserting civilization out of fear for your own survival will ensure its collapse, and is profoundly selfish. Selfishness and fear are a lot of what has created our current monumental crisis. They are not part of our salvation.

My hosts countered that civilization is obviously murderous to the planet, and attempting to wean themselves from it is, in their perspective, the only sane thing to do. Certainly a large part of Tod and Talia's motivation for living the way they do comes from not just a desire to survive any potential civilizational collapse, but also from a deeply felt love for nature. This love is expressed by rediscovering the basic knowledge that allowed humanity to survive sustainably for thousands of generations and, most importantly, in dedicating much of their time to teaching these skills to others. Ultimately, the differences in our separate responses — Tod and Talia's retreat to a more basic existence and my own move to the city — result from the same motivation to save what's left of the natural world but we have starkly divergent estimates of how capable humanity is in adapting itself to a more resource-limited world. Time will ultimately tell who is right.

Working on getting the firewood together and examining the ongoing construction like Tod and Talia's new sleeping quarters reminded me of how satisfying and empowering it is to labor at one's own survival. This is especially true, if, like me, you were molly-coddled as a child in a warm and secure suburban environment, where buildings were always comfortable, showers were always hot and there was always gas in the car to motor down to soccer practice. The empowerment generated by increasing one's self-sufficiency can be addictive, and it offers diminishing marginal returns as your self-sufficiency increases. Whereas growing some of your own food and providing some of your own fuel is extremely rewarding at lifting your self-esteem, I've fallen into the trap, like others I've seen, of taking this notion to its logical extreme of attempting to be entirely self-sufficient. Such behavior is anti-social and ultimately preposterous. While complete dependence on others is awful and usually puts folks on a fast track to being manipulated and abused, often to the point of volunteer slavery, attempting to be completely self-sufficient is often rightly interpreted as anti-social. And besides, what if you break your leg? Or, as often happens, get old? Better to embrace some independence, and then share your expertise on buildings, energy, food or what have you, with your surrounding community.

As it got dark and cold, we all headed to the common house, where Talia cooked us dinner. I had brought a few beers with me and the conversation got a little loose and energetic, touching on many of the philosophical points I've already written about in this chapter. When I think of primitivism, I think of hunting, especially with a bow and arrow. Told we were eating venison stew, I inquired if the deer had been hunted locally. As I shoveled spoonfuls of the stew into my mouth, they told me the deer had been hunted locally, but instead of being killed on the property it was retrieved from the dumpster behind a game butchering center in a nearby burg. The eyes, tongues and brains of discarded deer heads were the main ingredient in our stew. "How do you tell the good meat from the bad?" I naively inquired, chewing thoughtfully on some unidentified morsel in my mouth. Turns out the bad head meat often has glazed-over eyeballs and is covered in maggots. Simple enough, right? I finished my bowl of stew, which did, in fact, taste good, but I didn't go back for seconds. Fortunately, Talia had fried up a huge pile of acorn and corn flatcakes in bear fat, and I had my fill of those, not bothering to inquire about the origin of the bear.

The next morning was the start of another magical autumn day ablaze with color and the rustling of falling leaves. I headed towards the common house, genuinely excited by the prospect of another bagel smeared in bear fat. I was the first one up, and the fire was out. One of my many weaknesses is an entrenched addiction to coffee, and although I had a lighter in my pocket, I knew starting the morning fire with it would be a desecration. There I was with my camping espresso maker in hand and some fresh fair trade organic coffee grounds in a little brown bag, the sweat of the drug addict starting to break out across my forehead as I realized I was the only camp resident without the knowledge and capacity to start a fire in the traditional method. Kelly, a young man of Haitian extraction who had spent the last two years traveling and learning primitive skills, finally awoke and brought out his bow-drill fire starting kit. Did I want to try? Of course! I would be my own Prometheus, pulling the magic of fire from a collection of dried sticks. I began twirling the stick with my right hand in the bow between a stone socket, held in my left hand, on a fireboard with a notch cut in the side to catch the ember. After five or so exhausting minutes amid a gathering crowd of primitivists who wanted to see if the civilization-addicted writer would be able to pull it off, I finally had enough of an ember to plop it in the bird's nest, a collection of dried grass that would turn the ember into actual fire. I held this in my hands as I walked over towards the teepee of kindling stacked in the firepit, blowing gently until sparks and then finally flame sprung into life. I placed the flaming bird's nest under the kindling teepee and watched with pride and amazement as the flames spread. I was no longer a fire virgin, and I would be able to cook up my drugs! It was going to be a good day.

I left around lunch, managing to free the rental car without any noticeable damage, with Kelly riding shotgun. We'd talked quite a bit and he was interested in moving from a primitivist lifestyle to one engaged more in sustainable agriculture. It so happened that I have some friends at a place called Circle Acres down in the flatlands that is perhaps the perfect halfway house for primitivists converting to a more community-focused farming lifestyle, and I gave them a call to see if they'd be willing to take in a traveler for a while if he'd help them finish their cob home. We arrived around dusk and sat around the fire drinking mead and telling tales. The folks at Circle Acres practice many of the same primitivist skills as up at Wildroots, such as brain tanning and primitive fire starting, but they also engage more actively as farmers in the local food economy. It was good to be reminded of the fact that there's a thousand different ways to approach every issue, and one group wasn't necessarily right (or wrong) just because they took it to more of an extreme than another. With so many questions on what, eventually, will be sustainable, it's heartening to know there are so many different seekers of this elusive path.

I had learned earlier that summer that anarchism isn't always intentionally green. After my visit to the Firefly gathering in the mountains of North Carolina in July, I headed west, a few young hitchhikers in tow, to visit an anarchist squat in a mid-sized Midwestern city I promised to keep unnamed. I traded a few e-mails and phone calls with one of the principal members of the squat, whom I'll call Dave. He was unsure of the relevance of his squat to the purpose of my book, and admittedly, it wasn't entirely clear to me what I was interested in. How does one explain or justify curiosity? One thing that had intrigued me, upon hearing about the squat from a mutual friend, was some of the ecologically minded rehabs they'd done to the squat, like composting toilets and edible forest gardens. My hopes were that they were motivated by a strain of green anarchism that could repopulate our urban wastelands and transform them into grassroots ecological Edens.

To some extent, my wishes were fulfilled, although the situation turned out, not surprisingly, to be more complicated that my initial fantasies. Not much more than a mile away from a downtown that had benefited from massive redevelopment dollars in the form of museums and giant sports complexes, I pulled into the dead-end block of the squat. The neighborhood was a mix of small turn-of-the-century clapboard houses and fancy brick town homes, many with roofs missing and skeletonized by fire, and open lots where houses had once stood, many overgrown, others with tended gardens. Dave and his roommate and co-conspirator, whom I'll call Roger, lived in one of these smaller wood houses, without permission. Across the street, some friends and ideological sympathizers rented a three-story town home. This is where I camped out for my stay. A third building at the end of the dead end, also a three-story town home, was in the process of being clandestinely fixed up for more folks to move into.

Three or four other homes remained standing on the block, all of which looked relatively inhabitable (i.e., roofs still in existence). At least two had occupants of some variety. These neighbors were friendly and open, at least as much as could be hoped for in the sweltering 100-degrees-plus heat wave, and certainly seemed to bear no grudge against members of the collective. The first thing I noticed after I met Dave and he led me inside his home was the loud whir of window air conditioning units in his home. Where was this electricity coming from and what were their attitudes toward using this typically polluting energy, generally only available from The Man? Time would tell.

The interior of the home was comfortable, if modest, with a punkish, grad-school décor of music and political posters on the walls and stacks of books piled up on shelves, typical of many twenty-somethings' dwellings. For heat in the winter they'd built a full-sized rocket stove, with the heated cob bench started but not completed. It wouldn't be needed for a few months, at the earliest. Roger sat still on a worn-out couch, tall and thin in contrast to Dave's darker, stouter

The rocket stove inside the squat. It wasn't needed on the 100-degrees-plus days I was there.

frame. He didn't rise from his seat and barely looked up from the book he was reading, mumbling in an obviously suspicious way when I was introduced. I was not being welcomed with open arms into the squat. My presence, for now at least, was barely tolerated. I had yet to introduce my three tag-along hitchhikers, and I was unsure if they would be a help or a hindrance.

Fortunately, we were being put up across the street in the rented apartment where the atmosphere was more convivial. The two owners were traveling, but an eclectic mix of like-minded musicians and activists were busy in the kitchen, turning that year's harvest of cabbage into kimchi. I drank some wonderful ginger mead as the cabbage and carrots were chopped. The heat was exhausting, and this small taste of alcohol made me badly want a cold beer or two, a desire that arises with almost unerring exactitude every day at five o'clock, and often before. After I voiced my desire, Roger, the tall thin taciturn one, offered to walk me down to the beer store. I couldn't tell if he was warming up to me, or was merely bemused at my asinine drug dependency, and merely wanted to lead me around to feel superior. Honestly, as long as there was a cold beer waiting for me at the end of it, I didn't really care.

We set out into the dusk. After a minute or two, Roger perked up and began telling me about the neighborhood and their involvement with it. They had lived in their squat for almost four years, quite an accomplishment, and had barely escaped some close calls from the authorities. Much of the surrounding area was owned by a single developer, all told almost 40,000 properties, almost a third of the entire city. The developer was trying to get massive city, state and federal funding to rework the entire area in several stages. Such a project could easily run into the billions of dollars. Everything would be bulldozed and made into homogenous condo developments for a burgeoning middle class interested in living an urban life.

The plan sounded preposterous. Granted, I wasn't necessarily getting the unbiased story from my anarchist interlocutor, but follow-up research verified the rough outline of the scenario. Here was a city that had lost half of its population over the last few decades, and was still sliding. The idea that young families would be drawn to live in a condofied wasteland just because it was close to downtown seemed woefully naive. If my own experience back in Durham is any guide, it's the eclectic mix of historic housing and walkability, along with a proximity to a vibrant downtown, that seems to be the chief motivator for folks to move into cities. As we plodded towards the beer store, the afternoon heat finally abating slightly, we saw plenty of amazing homes waiting to be restored, although economic decline had resulted in a very disheartening activity — brick theft. Apparently, much of the arson was the result of thieves wanting to get access to the historic bricks, prized for their character. After being poached, they were then shipped off to the suburbs in the hopes of lending a bit of charm to an otherwise stale existence.

The quest for beer proved fruitless. The owners of the store were on vacation, and even the nearby gas station was dry, due to some obscure liquor law. I survived the sweltering night without it, if only just barely.

The next day Dave showed me around a few other squats, the Catholic Worker house, and a large urban garden squat members tended. All told there were roughly seven members of the squat,

The house on the right is maintained (but not owned) by a bunch of lawless anarchists. The one on the left is owned (but not maintained) by a capitalist developer.

occupying four houses without permission, a breakdown of six males and one female, all under the age of thirty, and all white. They were all friendly and open minded, and it was easy to bond talking about things I knew a lot about. I gave away two copies of my book and threw out ideas for obscure perennials like pawpaws and cardoons, tips on improved rainwater collection, slipstraw insulation, all topics safely out of the realm of politics. This goodwill won me the favor of an interview with four of them that afternoon, allowing me to delve deeper into their motives and philosophy. The group spent their time working on their homes, gardening, traveling, salvaging food out of dumpsters and doing the occasional paid work or work trade, things like baking for a local collectively-owned bakery or bicycle repair.

Collecting a coherent political philosophy from a group of anarchists is about as easy as herding feral cats, but it's possible to make a few generalizations about this particular bunch. Surprisingly, ecological motives were practically nonexistent. The idea that individual actions, such as using fewer fossil fuels or embracing organic gardening, would result in any substantial change in the broader environment was dismissed as bleeding-heart naiveté. Not unexpectedly, they had a deep vein of cynicism regarding the collusion of government and big business. What I found amazing was that rather than being crippled by it, this group was able to use their disgust for the entrenched political economic system as a source of motivation to steer their own personal lives towards self-sufficiency, so as to be as little tainted by the system as possible. While they had discovered and implemented many of the same regenerative systems as I had back in North Carolina, such as composting toilets, old building reuse and rainwater collection, to name just a few, they took no satisfaction from the idea that they were practically living paragons of ecological sustainability. Instead, their motives seemed to be motivated purely by personal independence. Nothing I said made them feel any sense of pride for their accomplishments in any kind of ecological framework.

A large vegetable garden, with beehive and compost bin, reclaimed from an abandoned lot. Despite having little interest in sustainability, the squatters had adapted a great many ecologically sound habits in the name of personal independence.

What about the air conditioners? Given the torrid heat, even ardent environmentalists like myself often resort to this most wonderful of devices. But the cool, fall-like air in their home was taking some serious watt-hours, burning at least a few pounds of coal an hour just to keep it humming. The electricity, it turns out, was stolen using a manipulated electrical meter. Using as much of this stolen juice as possible was seen as just another way of sticking it to The Man, regardless of any detrimental effect it might have on the climate, the same as getting free food from the dumpster or using scrap pallets to heat their homes with rocket stoves in the winter. Questioning the logic of their excessive electricity consumption proved fruitless.

Another source of encroaching gentrification came from a few blocks away, where someone was spending big money rehabbing a section of storefronts, and a handful of historic homes had been restored. After discovering this area on a random walk, I came back to the squat full of worries. The group had put so much work into repairing their abandoned homes and bringing the neighborhood back to life. How were they going to stop their hard work from being co-opted and basically stolen, once the gentrification made it a few more blocks over, and someone with a little money decided to get rid of them? They basically dismissed this unpleasant topic with the imperiousness of youth.

If this city actually wanted to fix up its housing and turn itself back into a vibrant living community, all it had to do was give away its abandoned housing to the young. Here were incredibly energetic twenty-somethings working to fix up the city's decaying infrastructure without even a hope of permanence. I drove out of that city with a smile on my face, thinking that these "anarchists" were actually what I would consider model citizens helping to rebuild their devastated neighborhood. Yet the powers that be held on to the hope of eventually kicking them all out and knocking down all those empty homes for "redevelopment." There's lots of potential here, but only if the ossified attitudes of those in power can somehow be made fluid again to allow the citizens of the city to rebuild it from the ground up.

═══════ Interview with Tod of Wildroots ═══════

Q: When I visited Wildroots, you said, "Whenever we use metal, we have an unfair advantage over nature." Yet you have an interest in blacksmithing and making tools. What do you consider to be a level of technology that works with nature over the long term?

A: I probably should have said something like "...over the *rest* of nature." Since I guess anything that happens on this planet is arguably "natural." Philosophy aside, it seems to me that only true stone-age technology is sustainable in the long term. Melting metals takes lots of energy. Energy comes from...? Trees, coal, etc. Not just energy but power, that is, lots of energy delivered fast. And no "green" or "renewable" or "sustainable" energy (like photovoltaics) is actually green, renewable or sustainable.

But that's all philosophizing. As a product of modern, high-tech civilization, I am unable to survive without at least metal tools. Maybe I can do fine without cars and electricity — but not without metal hand tools like axes and knives. Plus, I don't want to. I don't really want to put in all the effort it would take to be able to live one hundred percent in agreement with my philosophically arrived at ideals — it's too much work. And the ecosystems that sustained stone-age humans are gone. Too many extinctions, too much pollution, too many laws telling me what I can and can't harvest and when, where I can and can't go, etc. We modern humans have evolved into a species that is incapable of living sustainably and in harmony with our world. I am one of these creatures. I don't have an answer for all of us, but I can learn to cut back on the activities that don't make sense to me... philosophically.

Q: Keeping in mind that the long-term goal of Wildroots is self-sufficiency, tell me your thoughts about living off of today's consumerist society's prodigious waste.

A: We are continuously cutting back on our dumpster diving for food because, one, we wind up eating lots of shitty, chemical- and salt- and sugar-drenched crap that we otherwise wouldn't eat and two, because we think it's all going away so we don't want to be dependent on it. But we like the yummy gifts of mother dumpster and we are not capable — right now — of self-sufficiency. So we live off the fat of the land.

Q: Tell me about the motivation for abandoning mainstream society and living here.
A: I wish it were true that I have abandoned mainstream society — but I haven't. I still drive. I have a phone. I have friends and family that I won't abandon, etc. I've moved to the fringes, that's all.

As to why: I guess it comes down to the simple realization that, to me, mainstream society makes no sense. With virtually every single action we take as members of the modern economic society — whether it be buying a solar panel or dropping bombs, we are destroying ourselves and our planet. I live in a beautiful, clean valley. I don't want it to be destroyed. But in order for me to have any modern products, some beautiful place must be destroyed for a factory to be built or powered or for raw materials to be removed. That thought makes me feel sad and guilty — and it *is* sad and I *am* guilty of complicity in my own self-destruction when I participate in any way in the economy. So I want to minimize those feelings of sadness and guilt. So I'm trying to learn skills that allow me to live with more peace in my heart. Pretty selfish, really.

Q: What do you see as the long-term goal of Wildroots?
A: Long-term goal? As I learn the depths of my own ignorance as far as true self-sufficiency, my own long-term goals become more and more nebulous. I guess I just want to become less and less dependent on high-tech shit. And also I want to, as much as I can, unprogram my highly programmed mind. This societal programming is another thing that becomes clearer to me the longer I'm here.

Q: What kind of political structure do you think would work best (e.g., to manage interpersonal conflicts, resource use, etc.)?
A: No fucking idea. I have no political leanings and I guess I just don't

think its an important thing *for me* to think about. How about a "responsibilitocracy"? Nah, as soon as something gets a label it gets followers and believers and it gets fucked up.

Q: After six years of studying, you've acquired a respectable set of ancient skills, such as fire making and hide tanning. How did you acquire these skills, and what others are you working on currently (or hope to in the near future)?
A: Skills are acquired through immersion. I have taken classes and gone to primitive skills gatherings and taken more classes. The classes give me a starting point. From there, living a life in which these skills are used every day has given me some real proficiency.

Q: Explain the process of the brain tan.
A: The animal is skinned then the flesh and fat and as much membrane as possible are scraped off the flesh side. Then the hair is "slipped" or removed. This can be done by rotting the hide in water or soaking it in a lye solution of wood ashes or drain opener.

The hide is then saturated with a brain solution. This can be actual brains stirred into warm water or egg yolks. Some people add a bit of oil or soap to make the solution penetrate better. The solution is squeegeed or wrung out of the hide. The saturation/squeegeeing is repeated two or three times. Then the hide is stretched as it dries. When it is completely dry, if it is not as soft as desired, the whole process can be repeated until the desired softness is attained. Finally, the hide is smoked. This sets the process — if the hide gets wet before it is smoked, it will dry crunchy. After the smoking it will be soft after a bit of stretching if it gets wet.

Q: Some people who are familiar with the neo-primitivism movement have mentioned they thought there was an atmosphere of competition to see how tough you could be by, for example, eating road kill or dumpster diving deer heads. Can you speak to this? To what extent do we as people need to cultivate our "toughness" to survive in the future?

A: I think that, as a bunch of soft, pampered, civilized folks, we do need to become tougher. I think we do need to challenge ourselves emotionally and physically. There certainly is that kind of competition — particularly among younger people. But I like it because I learn a lot about what can and can't be done.

And is there anything actually "tough" about eating perfectly good meat — just because it was killed by a car? Or does it make me tough to get free food from a dumpster instead of going inside? I don't think so. Many of us enjoy the shock value. But I feel like I live a pretty lush and comfortable life.

What about other forms of toughness? Like seeing all the dead animals we killed with our cars and not being heartbroken. It is sad and unutterably wasteful and stupid and hard hearted. And any of us who drive accept the fact that cars kill animals. Even if I can't remember the last time I killed an animal with a car, I'm complicit because I know it can happen.

And we need — all of us in modern society — to be able to, for instance, hear about all the people we're killing in Pakistan and Afghanistan...and just go about our lives. Mountains are destroyed so we can have electricity — and we keep using it. We have to be tough enough to harden our hearts to the stupendous, self-destructive damage we are causing by living the way we do. That's pretty tough. And it's a kind of toughness I don't want.

Speaking for myself and, I think for many others in the "neo-primitivist movement" (or whatever people want to label it — how about "neo-self-reliant"?), I do want to be tougher than the average soft-ass American and I also want to be less wasteful and less dependent on fuckheads and corporations to keep me alive.

9

Community Rehab

ERHAPS ONE OF THE MOST profound questions humanity
faces this century is whether cities are sustainable. The neces-
sity to transition away from fossil fuels is blatantly obvious because of
their dwindling supply and planet-killing nature, yet cities and even
smaller towns depend on a constant flow of resources from not just
the surrounding countryside but all over the world, made possible
primarily because of the colossal amount of energy stored in oil, coal
and natural gas. But cities also offer the chance for residents to take
advantage of economies of scale and the availability of necessities that
those in suburban and exurban areas don't have. Living in the hive, so
to speak, allows for the option of dispensing with the automobile, living in co-housing that is much more energy efficient than stand-alone
homes, and the ability to transport goods in large quantity to these
hubs of commerce. Unlike starting from scratch in new communities like Sanctuary and The Farm, huge quantities of infrastructure
already exists that are either quite efficient or carry the potential to be
retrofitted for sustainability relatively easily. To deal with the masses
of people that already populate the planet, and who will continue to
do so for the foreseeable future unless some really awful shit goes
down (not out of the question, unfortunately), we quite simply *must*

figure out a way to make our cities work without fossil fuels. While the neo-primitivists like those I visited in the previous chapter have much to teach us about how to live a life more integrated with nature and the available resources of our surrounding ecology, the prospect of giving up on the billions in urban environments is too terrible to contemplate. Fortunately, there are some brilliant and inspired folks who are experimenting with how to do this all across the land, regardless of what the law stipulates or the potential disdain generated by the outdated mores of the disconnected urban mindset.

It might seem that adopting radical techniques and methods to achieve sustainability in an urban environment would make you a ripe target for the powers that be to squash you like a bug under their jackboot. But from my own experience and from those I visited in this chapter, it's often the paradox that the larger the city you're working in, the easier it is to operate with a kind of impunity and anonymity, assuming you don't bother your neighbors. In many ways, cities are our species' highest achievement, being repositories of culture, hubs of intense creativity and platforms for a huge diversity of peoples to freely associate and pursue a great variety of interests. On some level, cities have to adopt a laissez-faire attitude simply as a fact of economics. While I'm sure there are plenty of rich elites who would love to install a police state in urban environments the way they do in their gated communities, law enforcement often has more pressing matters than worrying about whether someone has some livestock they're not supposed to, is adding a green roof or some solar heating equipment to their home without permits or is turning a residential intersection into a community hangout by building cob tea stands on the sidewalk. Unlike in smaller towns or rural areas where anything weird going on is big news, in urban environments if you're not mugging someone or selling crack on the corner, you can usually get away with some cool shit, at least for a while. And if your city is Detroit, well then hell, you can pretty much do whatever you want.

My former wife and I made the big decision to move to the city after our country life, centered around our Waldenesque solar cob home, turned out to require fantastic amounts of driving. You might have thought we would have learned our lesson, since even our cob house, squirreled away as it was deep in the woods, had ultimately been found out by the inspector. Now ensconced on a main thorough-fare a half mile from the downtown inspector's office, we nevertheless carried out a variety of renovations, all of which should have required at least signing our names on some piece of paper and handing over a not so nominal fee. Most obviously, we installed a green roof and a modestly sized PV system that changed the structural nature of the roof and should likely have had an engineer's stamp. More daring was our humanure composting in our backyard. Sandwiched as we were between a fancier older neighborhood and lots of apartments filled with lots of Latin American immigrants, I never noticed anyone look askance at the large four-foot by four-foot compost bin of decompos-ing poo just five feet from the street. The young urban professionals were too busy pointing out the cute chickens to the toddler in the stroller they were pushing.

With visions of clandestine humanure dancing around in my head, I was very excited to make the acquaintance of Nance Klehm up in Chicago and discover that I would be arriv-ing just when she was bringing her Hum-ble Pile project to a close. Nance is an ex-tremely creative and hardworking lady and a paragon of integrity. More performance artist than activist, she has a take-no-shit attitude (actually a take-*your*-shit one) that initially comes across as bristly, but be-comes friendly and finally profoundly in-spirational once you get through her tough exterior. Nance invited me to accompany her around the city on bike as she returned a portion of a variety of friends' crap they had so generously donated two years back — composted, of course. I borrowed a bike from the friends I was staying with and we hit the mean streets of Chicago just

Nance Klehm provides some direc-tion during "The Great Giveback," part of raising awareness about the possibilities of integrating our bodies into the urban ecology of Chicago.

as rush hour was getting fierce, Nance pulling her trailer with a few hundred pounds of composted poop wrapped up in fancy hand-sewn bags with a silk-screened drawing of an intestine on the side, me following behind trying to do my part by keeping the rumbling traffic far enough away from the goods to not cause any accidental tipping, which would probably result in the entire city's Hazmat squad setting up a ten-block cordon if any composted poop spilled. This part of the Humble Pile project was called "The Great Giveback," and true to her flair for attention-grabbing stunts, Nance had arranged for a pair of reporters to meet us at the first stop, a cute bungalow in a shady neighborhood tucked up against a community garden.

The recipient of this amazing gift was a woman in her early forties with a young daughter tucked inside peeking out through the window at all the commotion. Nance had done a good job of selecting a wide variety of fairly conventional Chicagoans to volunteer to collect their ordure in five-gallon buckets over the course of a month, with Nance showing up (by truck this time, the raw product is much heavier) to take the unwanted "waste" back to her south-side spread where she could transform it into its desirable end product, the foundation for healthy soil and hence all life. Shit happens, just like the bumper stickers say, but the great thing is that compost just happens too, if you

"Wait a minute, this isn't poop!" The pooch quickly lost interest in the composted manure. The plants in the community garden next door, however, were definitely salivating.

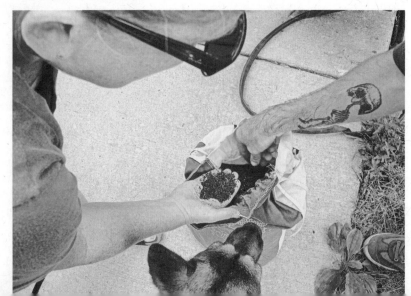

go to a little bit of trouble to set up the right conditions. In my own experience, watching my smelly turds become slowly transformed into rich, dark humus, applying that to my fruit trees, and then plucking a pear or persimmon that I knew was nourished from own body has done more to help me understand that I am a part of the cycle of life than any other single event or activity. I was inspired into action by Joe Jenkins' *The Humanure Handbook*, one of the most fascinating reads you'll ever pick up (and perhaps the ultimate bathroom book) — as fun, on some level, as reading about sex or eating — and finally understanding how fascinating our bodies are and what makes them tick.

It was some of this wonder that Nance was trying to instill in her Humble Pile volunteers and, through the media coverage, everyone else in Chicago. When the pink bow on the yellow and brown bag was untied, it was almost impossible for everyone there not to stick their hand in and grab some. You knew it was no longer shit when the pooch showed up, gave the bag a big sniff, and then went away, not the least bit interested in peeing on the bag or eating a big mouthful. For city dwellers used to relieving themselves in some good old-fashioned drinking water and then watching it spiral away into some forgotten no man's land, the effect was surely revolutionary. By engaging in these spectacles, Nance is able to bring attention to the fact that she operates in this sustainable way on an ongoing basis at her Southside spread, and offers an invitation to others to consider participating in a similar way.

This is just one of a great variety of projects that Nance has been engaged in over the last decade, not just in Chicago but all over the States and Europe. Currently these are documented on her two websites, spontaneousvegetation.net and salvationjane.net. One of my favorites of the many projects profiled, because I have a love of food trucks, solar ovens and rocket stoves, is Ramblin' Range, that she performed in Copenhagen. This reminded me of Ed's Solar Cafe, but in portable form. Nance pulled a large solar oven around by bike, cooking veggie tacos and feeding the masses. The cloudier climate necessitated back-up heat from a rocket stove. Nance then recorded a bunch

Nance juices some pears from the harvest. Her urban homestead in Southside Chicago is a model for integrating ecological principles into our daily lives.

of the conversations that occurred during these taco feasts and posted them on her website.

═══ Interview with Nance Klehm ═══

Q: You take a very holistic approach to the many problems facing humanity, encompassing issues of food, social justice and ecological integration. For example, your involvement with Greenhouses of Hope helps not only feed the homeless and the hungry but teaches participants about the cycles of nature. Can you talk about this project and concept? How successful has it been so far, in your opinion?

A: Two of the guys I've trained at the Greenhouse are still there — both of them sober for over two years. They have the best horticultural training I know of. They run the 5,000 square feet of greenhouse, the outdoor vegetable garden, the pollinators garden, the houseplants within the entire institution, the street trees and sidewalk landscape and the several million worms that drive it all, plant propagations by seed, cuttings and division, they are trained in masonry and carpentry, pruning, composting, etc.

This idea started when I was asked to help the Mission come up with a greenhouse and a greenhouse program at the new facility they were building. They are in the business of getting people sober. They are evangelicals. In other words they are busy and didn't see the connection between their spiritual beliefs and ecology. Although interested in the project, they were worried that this greenhouse would distract them from their goals and cost them a huge amount of money to maintain. My pitch was that they could use the greenhouse to recycle the waste generated by the 2,000 meals a day served in the cafeteria as well as newspaper and cardboard through a vermiculture system. We started with a worm population of 30,000 and nothing in the greenhouse. In six months, we had enough castings (nine tons!) to grow thousands of seedlings and by the end of the first year we had tropicals and succulents, veggies and herbs in the outdoor garden and on the roof. After a year, we started selling our worms and making small wormeries from scavenged oak pallets to sell also.

The vermiculture system is large, millions of worms and all maintained by hand. We chop up hundreds of pounds of food slop at a time and feed the worms by the shovelful. When residents come in, they are amazed at the transformational power of the worms — how fast they go through the waste.

The program helps the residents who live and work there learn patience and develop long-term planning and basic nurturing skills. It is a place of reflection and very demanding physically and mentally — such a complexity! But everyone who is assigned there loves it. The Greenhouses are attached to the building — one is seen by the entire cafeteria and the other by the overnight guests in the warming room.

Q: Unlike a lot of permaculture teachers out there, you often use art, both visual and performance, to challenge students and viewers to get us to think about some of the deeper questions and assumptions underpinning our way of life. Can you talk about the role art plays in your work? For instance, *Humble Pile* is a kind of performance piece that gets us to rethink the concept of "waste" and natural cycles. What was the genesis for this idea?

A: I use artistic strategies to reenergize or reawaken dialogues or broaden audience discussion around issues that are important to me. My approach is playful and humorous and accessible. My audience is broad, from DIY crusties to Latino immigrants, to DIY moms, to conservative evangelicals. So it is not only my visual presentation and performance, but the way I language around the dialogue of things that I create strategies for. So many things that are important to me have become LITE'ND by "green progressives" who follow marketing BS and are not critical or deeply embodied. I don't want people to shut down or drop out or shop more because of how these issues and connections are languaged around.

Q: When you say "LITE'nd," you mean…?
A: They take the high energy fuel or fat out of it. They can only consume the slim diet version.

Q: One of the issues you tackle that is dear to my heart is the integration of nature with existing urban environments, through foraging, forest gardens, humanure composting, etc. I know you're more peripatetic lately, but you lived for a long time in Chicago. Tell me about some of the successes and challenges you had in your neighborhood there. What motivated you to move on?
A: I love my Little Village neighborhood in Chicago. It is a low-to-no-income Mexican immigrant neighborhood. (I'm the "white lady.") People are still connected to land (former campesinos) or only one generation away from land — with a strong cooking culture at home, growing vegetables and herbs in buckets or directly in soils, keeping chickens and rabbits…or they've got informal economies of food preparation, such as tamales, etc., or car mechanics, carpentry, masonry, etc. It's a village mentality…there's informal exchanges on the street, bartering of services, paying later when you don't have the cash

on you…people are interdependent. They recognize this and reinforce it with their behaviors. It is also rough — the Latin Kings are
strong, I hear shootings and see guns, I'm sure some of my neighbors
are illegal. It is *loud* in the summers — it has its own soundtrack of hip
hop and ranchero music from cars and houses. This neighborhood is
more connected than almost any other neighborhood that my friends
live in — it functions as a village mentality.

Successes — I was able to turn my yard into a forest due to this informal village mentality. My neighbors love my chickens and quail —
adore the rooster, rabbit and fish. They ask me questions about food,
cook for me, we exchange tools, etc.

I have a side yard and several sites on which I grow or am allowed
to gather from. On my roof, I have a sleeping structure, a greenhouse,
a medicinal meadow and some fruit trees.

Q: Many sustainability activists bump into legal restrictions that im-
pede their work in some way. To what extent has the legality of your
activities been an issue? How much is the law on your mind generally
as something that inhibits our transition to a more sustainable existence?

A: I think we need to weigh in on policy — by going to meetings,
speaking out, writing, organizing but only as long as we also create the
living models that become the new, more grounded practice. Many
of these living models that are embodied practice are either not by
the books, or condoned, or are simply, blatantly illegal. I work with
nature's law, metabolic law, holistic system law — however you want
to call it. I don't think we should wait for policy to catch up to what
needs to happen.

Yes indeed, cities are not systems thinking, but separately "sys-
temed." And it is this sort of grouping of disconnected systems that
inhibit this transition. Which shouldn't inhibit the actions you take
towards living an ecological lifestyle. One simply has to recognize the
risks. If I get arrested for composting, just because what I am composting is human waste (or for owning a rooster or having a still, or
whatever) well then that would be great press. Healthy soil is part of

the biological infrastructure all of life depends on. Right? I mean, who and what are we working for anywho???

Q: You've been active in the field of permaculture for a while now. What is your sense of the momentum of the movement today and its strengths and weaknesses?

A: I don't use the terms "sustainability" or its derivatives. I don't use the term "permaculture" when I talk about my work, because it is not where my heart or actions originated. I live in relation to this world and learn from listening and interacting with it.

This is about developing an intimacy with land, self and other life forms. This is about creating and supporting healthy habitat for all living creatures. This is about having a relationship. This is about abundance.

I think permacultural thinking is a great help towards working with and building natural systems. But it should be recognized, the principles are not new. It is already how many people grow and think about their interaction with land. People who realize that their lives are dependent on working with natural systems already do it. These are largely the landed poor, the societally disenfranchised, the indigenous. Heck! I am repeating myself.

I think permaculture as a movement is too branded and self-referencing to be interesting in and of itself. Permaculture Design Courses are general overviews, completed quickly and graduates take their show on the road without having spent years cutting their teeth on a site/group/process. It is treated as a theoretical exercise or the perfect planning tool. But the proof is always in the quality of execution and the continued commitment to a place and people. When you see the permaculture guru in the middle of the road, kill him. Because, indeed, it is usually a "him".

Q: Anything else you're dying to say. Poo fear and body hatred aside...

A: *Embrace your body as a soilmaker. Loop your nutrient.*

Urban policy lacks the underpinning of true systematic thinking.

Cities understand their water systems, waste systems, industrial systems, food systems, education systems, etc. as independent systems that only peripherally interact with one another. Soil and water are seen as stuff to move around as opposed to something to celebrate, take care of and revere as foundations of life.

There is a very crucial difference between creating a positive outcome and managing to prevent a negative outcome. Policy is set on surviving in the short term instead of thriving through the long term.

Urban policy makers as well as citizens seem to follow "preventative management." Cities create best practices or ordinances around composting that don't allow for further abundance and education. Why don't we trust ourselves and our neighbors and friends to learn about and adopt such ancient technologies that create abundant health? Does the disconnect from ourselves run too deeply?

There have been systems of building and nurturing soil fertility since the beginning of agriculture that we have only recently dropped from our food system. Up until the 1930s farmers who came to Chicago with their produce and meats filled their wagons with the city residents' toilet waste to safely fertilize their fields. The biological economics of cycling were understood and valued.

Soil is not a resource, it is something we are in relation to.

Now urban soils are not only minerally depleted from continual disturbance, they are compacted, salinated and contaminated by heavy metals from our industries, our detergents, our lawn and garden sprays and our salt use in the wintertime. Most urban growers have a composting element and cover cropping, but they are also growing in raised beds with compost produced elsewhere and soil imported from surrounding outlying farms stripped of their topsoil when these farms are in turn forced out of business by expanding sprawl. And even reaching back further, these farms started the soil nutrient depletion cycle when they ripped up grass (deep rooted, perennial prairie grasses) and replaced it with other grass (the formerly sacred commodity known as corn, and genetically modified at that).

All soil comes out of the backside of some other organism: us, other mammals, reptiles, birds, insects, fish, fungi, bacteria. Shit is the beginning of the food cycle and the so-called end of it. How can we ignore such a simple and magical truth?

At the beginning of the *Humble Pile* Chicago project, I told the participants that they could either have their waste returned to them transformed or not. All of them were curious enough to receive some of it back, be part of The Great Giveback, and they received a sack of it that they then could use or gift as they wished. Needless to say, the 1,500 gallons of human waste that was collected for *Humble Pile* made a lot of compost and there is much remaining for me to share with others who are in need of "proof" and can use it to help urban lands.

Again, soil is not a resource, it is something we are in relation to.

And food is not a resource and eating is not an idea. It is a communion between organisms. The fact remains: our food is only as healthy and nutritious as the soil is that produces it.

Everything comes into this world hungry.

Everything flows towards soil.

More good times were to be had at the next stop on The Great Giveback, the home of a mechanical whiz whose specialty was retrofitting conventional bicycles into electric speedsters capable of going fifty miles an hour. After the humanure delivery, met with genuine appreciation but tempered by familiarity with the idea and end product, I got a tour of the wonderful little urban garden he had constructed in his backyard, complete with fruit trees of all varieties and a huge trellis overflowing with grape tomatoes, exotic melons and ripe grapes. I tried not to be too rude and greedy about stuffing some of these hard-won delicacies in my mouth while he went down into the basement to bring out his handcrafted electric bike to show off. I was about to have my socks blown off by his handiwork. I love electric bikes, at least in concept, as a means of making this form of transportation more accessible for those who otherwise might stick with the convenience of the wretched automobile. Bikes, including electric ones, can be more than 100 times more efficient in moving people around than cars (see my detailed analysis of this in my co-authored book *The Carbon-Free*

Home), yet many cyclists maintain a disdain for electric bikes that I find haughty and elitist. Unfortunately the options for electric bikes are nowhere near what the market would bear, as I can attest to from my own shopping experience. I must have spent a full week traveling around North Carolina going to specialty bike stores that carried electric bikes, trying them all to find the right model, during a year-long automobile sabbatical I was taking to see if carlessness was feasible for my life. All of them (close to a dozen) had some major issue, coupled with sky-high price tags, that made their purchase untenable. Some of the contempt that electric bikes seem to engender is probably from similar less-than-inspiring experiences. But in cultures where biking is thoroughly engrained as a means of transport by all classes, like China and the Netherlands, electric bikes are extremely popular. We're just not doing something right.

Embarrassingly, I ended up purchasing a very cheap Chinese model through the Northern Tool catalog to at least try and get a taste of living with one. It worked decently, for a while, until I left it unlocked when I went inside for a minute and came back out to find it gone. Ah, yes, the problem with bikes is that they are their own get-away vehicle, making them perhaps the easiest thing in the world to steal. But what really got my goat was that I hadn't put the battery in the bike yet and this particular model was very heavy, so using it without its electric power was nearly impossible. I'm sure Mr. or Ms. Bicycle Thief dumped the thing in an alley not far away, but I never found it. So for now, my dreams of integrating an electric bicycle into my life remain just that.

Our host was trying to rectify this problem with his creations. A big issue with electric bikes is the 20 miles per hour cap that federal law stipulates, which sounds fast compared with regular biking but is still pretty pokey in practical terms of getting where you want to go in a timely fashion compared to a car. Starting from scratch means you can ignore this ninnyness and make a genuinely kick-ass electric bike. This one had enough lithium-ion batteries to give it around a 100 mile range (assuming some moderation in the speed department) and an overdrive mechanism that basically operated like a nitrous oxide injection in a race car, allowing a top sustained speed of 50 miles per hour. I couldn't wait to try it! My host was happy to saddle me up until he noticed this enthusiasm and began having second thoughts, fearing, no doubt, my early death and the ruination of his hard work, but I hopped on to show my determination before he could take it away. I never did kick it into overdrive, finding 35 miles per hour on a bike inside the city to be plenty scary, which is just as well, because I found out upon my return that I had been zooming up and down a one-way street. Fortunately, this was during a lull in traffic.

Bicycling was very much in evidence in the next urban environment I visited, Portland, Oregon. This city is renowned the world over for its progressive policies and embraces a commitment to sustainability probably second to none in the US. I had been cautiously impressed with my own burg's steps towards a nascent greenness, but once out of Dixie on the far away shores of the left coast, I realized old dirty Durham hasn't really done squat compared with some place like Portland. The problem with that, of course, is that if you happen to show up writing a book about underground sustainability, you've got kind of slim pickings, because a lot of the battles have already been fought and won. I visited a legal and very cute straw bale home built within the city limits, biked around on streets clearly marked with large bike signs and filled with speed humps to deter car traffic, and then parked said bike at an outdoor beer garden with the largest bike rack I've ever seen, almost full, and drank beer all afternoon in the August sun. I was trying to hunt down some folks from City Repair and get a tour of the (formerly) illegal street reclaiming they engaged in, but the weather was so nice and I had a lot of friends to catch up with over a cold brewski. Finally I scheduled a tour and had to shake off a good beer buzz and head over.

I was sure glad I did. The concept of street reclaiming is something I've read a lot about but haven't witnessed very much of. One of my favorite books is Bernard Rudofsky's *Streets for People: A Primer for Americans*, where he skewers the inhuman scale of both sprawled out burbs (too horizontal) and city blocks made hostile by oversized buildings (too vertical). He poetically compares these environments

Share-It Square in Portland, Oregon. This intersection was reclaimed, with the assistance of City Repair, through mural painting, a tea stand and a cob bench with a green roof, among other installations by the community.

with Bologna in Italy, where shorter buildings, covered walkways and plenty of public commons create a rich and vibrant urban environment that not only gives its residents a high standard of living but also draws tourists from all over the world to enjoy it. I'd also read a lot about the *woonerf* in Holland, basically neighborhood streets retrofitted to calm car traffic and provide a comfortable and pleasant outdoor space for city dwellers. Street reclaiming is catching on this side of the pond, and has both its conventional urban planning methods of implementation, as well as its more radical DIY guerrilla adherents. Regardless, the goal is to reclaim the street from the automobile and give it back to the citizen, supposedly who cities were built for in the first place.

City Repair certainly started out in the latter category of guerrilla-style street reclaiming. The first project they engaged in was what they term Intersection Repair, and the first intersection they repaired, and the one I visited, was at SE 9th Street and SE Sherrett Street, named Share-It Square, in the leafy neighborhood of Sellwood in southeast Portland. It has been maintained since 1996. The centerpiece of any Intersection Repair is the painting of a giant mural in the middle of the two cross streets. Other components, developed over time, may include cob benches, tea stands, wildflower plantings, children's' play areas, community bulletin boards and book exchange kiosks. Often some aspects of the "place-making" will spill over into neighbors' properties, with their blessing of course. Rather than doing the work themselves, City Repair acts as a facilitator once enough community interest is generated by neighborhood residents. Volunteers in the organization pride themselves on their horizontal organizational structure, so that rather than a hierarchy they have what they term a "chaordic," for "chaotically organized," system of governance, which is more egalitarian and organic. By bringing neighbors together to reclaim and beautify the intersection, they lay the foundation for community interaction that can then be maintained and expanded through this new public commons, what the ancient Greeks referred to as the agora. From the tales I heard on my two-hour-long tour, it seemed common for this place-making to bring to the surface disagreements that already existed in the neighborhood, so that an intersection repair can quickly become quite contentious. But rather than shy away from these disagreements, dealing with them is viewed as a needed healing process that must occur in order for any real sense of community to exist, and thus lays the foundation for dealing with more difficult issues — everything from gentrification to increased crime to racial discord — that might arise. Ideally, the intersection repair remains relatively lighthearted and fun, to help facilitate dealing with neighbors during these tougher times.

Whimsy, then, is an important aspect of both the giant mural in the center of the intersection and the other structures the neighbors decide to build. At Share-It Square there was a sculpted cob bench

Near Share-It Square, neighbors make cob as part of a house renovation, helping to bring ecological principles like natural building into an urban environment.

with a green roof and an almost-ripe fig growing around it, a tea stand maintained with hot tea and clean cups, a covered kids' play area made out of interlocking branches, another covered cob bench catty-corner to the original one, a book kiosk where neighbors deposited old magazines and books for others to peruse, and a very cute cob beehive thing with a door for opening up and putting something in (I have no idea what, a random present for a random passerby perhaps?). The intersection was painted with a large planet Earth where giant animals (like bunnies and puppies) were riding bicycles and unicycles around. It was very colorful, but I couldn't help but ask how long these things last, and I also couldn't help but notice the gutters on several corners of the intersection where loose paint would flow down every time it rained. I was told that the intersection starts to look pretty bedraggled after about a year and it's recommended that the neighborhood make intersection painting an annual event. Because of this relatively high maintenance, if enthusiasm wanes some

Intersection Repairs can fall on hard times and become something of an eyesore. The paint going down the gutter was a contentious topic among City Repair volunteers, but was viewed as a perhaps acceptable sacrifice to develop a deeper sense of community, although it's difficult to gauge the relative worth of such abstract principles as the health of a human community versus the health of the surrounding ecology. Ideally you wouldn't have to sacrifice one for the other. I have to say that, personally, I was very taken with the idea of the giant mural, but the maintenance aspect seemed too overwhelming for very many neighborhoods to keep up over the long haul. Probably the most practical aspect, and what seemed to be the most utilized during my short visit, were the benches that decorated the intersections and allowed weary bicyclists and pedestrians a chance to cool their heels and people watch. Humans being such social creatures, I wonder if there's not some people-watching critical mass that potentially feeds itself, where enough benches brings out enough people to watch each other and make the intersection an actual living, thriving place. My understanding is that the most effective traffic calming device is not brightly painted intersections, interesting architecture or strips of beautiful flowers, although all of these help, but pedestrians walking around, the sight of which dramatically lowers drivers' speeds.

City Repair's community-building and place-making facilitations underscore the crucial fact that even the largest of cities are merely an agglomeration of small villages, each of which requires its own public commons. Using public art like the intersection murals, social structures like benches and tea stands and ecological installations like cob benches and native flower gardens, reinstates that vital sense of human scale that Rudofsky identified as core to creating thriving urban environments where they have so frequently withered due to television, air conditioning and the general hectic pace of modern city life.

The history of the first Intersection Repair in the Sellwood neighborhood provides an interesting prototype for how underground sustainability can rise through the surface of outmoded regulation and become a legal force for good. Talking with the folks at City Repair, and rereading the excellent booklet *Making Their Own Plans* by Brett Bloom (who introduced me to Nance Klehm above and Ben and Kate in Chapter Two) and meeting Ava Bromberg gives a solid background for this pivotal moment in urban regeneration. In the spring of 1996, neighbors started gathering in a garden of fruit trees and flowers for what they dubbed "T-Hows," basically a time for the community to get together and drink tea and shoot the shit during the beautiful spring weather. After living amongst one another anonymously for years, neighbors found they enjoyed each other's company, and started planning events for the space: music, poetry readings and just general hanging out and drinking tea. The Bureau of Buildings heard about the gatherings, sometimes exceeding hundreds of people, and issued a directive for them to stop. Ultimately, all this did was provoke the neighbors to make a bolder move in reclaiming the part of their neighborhood that had been all but abandoned to the terrors of the automobile: the main intersection in the neighborhood. They planned to get a permit to block off the streets during a weekend day and paint a huge mural in the intersection to reclaim the space so long denied to pedestrians. Initially, they sought permission from the Portland Department of Transportation (PDOT) to legally paint the intersection, but were ultimately refused. Some sympathetic members of the PDOT offered a suggestion: ask forgiveness rather than ask permission. As the day of the block party approached, residents got together to secure supplies and finalize the design for their mural: colorfully painted concentric circles connecting the four corners of the intersection, to be named Share-It Square. In addition to the mural, the block party also put up the first tea stand, info kiosk and playhouse.

Almost immediately, PDOT requested that the installation be removed or else heavy fines would be levied against the neighbors involved. Instead of bristling, the neighbors stayed organized and engaged not only the authorities at PDOT but also sympathetic city council members, and began surveying residents of the neighborhood to gauge acceptance and watched the intersection to notice changes in traffic speeds, pedestrian use, general safety and crime activity. Quickly convinced of the effectiveness of the Intersection Repair in increasing livability and its overwhelming acceptance by neighbors, the city council and PDOT granted formal approval for the project. As City Repair formed from this and other activism in Portland, they worked over the next several years to craft legislation to provide for the legitimate creation of Intersection Repairs, and on September 19, 2001, City Ordinance #175937 was passed. In sum, the ordinance states the city will grant a revocable permit for intersection modifications if a petition of support is presented that states approval from each adjacent neighbor to the intersection and at least 80 percent of the residents on the project street(s) two blocks in each direction. The petition must include a written and illustrated description of the proposed changes and demonstrate how the project will maintain or improve traffic and pedestrian safety.

Intersection Repair is not the only activity that City Repair engages in. Besides educational workshops and advocacy, City Repair hosts an annual ten-day place-making event in late spring, called the Village Building Convergence, that started in 2000. As the name suggests, the idea is to strengthen the neighborhoods, or small villages, that make up the city, thereby creating community and empowering residents to take control of their city by focusing on their own streets. By concentrating neighborhood enhancement activity into this ten-day period, a much greater awareness and synchronicity can be created throughout the entire city. Participants visit other ongoing projects, host workshops and throw block parties to inspire and connect with one another. Almost anyone can offer a workshop on whatever topic they desire, be it on politics, building, health, community or whatever. The festival attracts out-of-town participants as well, hopefully helping to sow the seeds of place-making in other locales, and provides an excellent opportunity for cross-pollination among disciplines. Another focus of City Repair is Block Repair, where residents are encouraged to take down fences and open up more of their backyards as a shared space, basically building small parks that offer much more space and recreation for residents than their own individual plots of land, and strengthening neighborly relationships.

My next adventure in learning about how to transform our urban environments to steer them towards a sustainable rather than chaotic future came from Scott Kellogg and Stacy Pettigrew. I first became acquainted with their work when my former wife and I were on a cross-country book tour by train in 2008, promoting our book, *The Carbon-Free Home*, which contains DIY projects to retrofit existing homes to not use any fossil fuels. One of the biggest worries any author has while they are plugging away on a book idea is that there is someone out there who will beat you to the punch and put out a book on the same topic a few months before you do. Perusing the other recent releases at A Cappella Books on Moreland Avenue in Atlanta, I came across the title *Toolbox for Sustainable City Living*, and suspected serious competition. Fortunately, while there was some overlap, most of Scott and Stacy's book, detailing projects undertaken by the Rhizome Collective they spearheaded in Austin, Texas, focused more on food, waste and bioremediation compared to our book's focus on energy conservation and solar and other renewable energy. Still, it was very fascinating to see another couple out there working in such a similar vein, and my fear of being upstaged was quickly replaced by a desire to get in touch and find out more about them.

The opportunity presented itself when I discovered that the Austin project had folded its doors and the couple had moved to Albany, New York, to start over, not far from my friend Matt Bua's b-home spread up in the Catskills that I visited regularly. As opposed to the way things had played out for City Repair in Portland, here was a collective promoting urban sustainability that had flouted the law and then paid the ultimate price — they'd been completely evicted and shutdown, and in what might be argued to be as liberal and progressive a city as Portland. Obviously, sometimes when you act first and ask forgiveness later, you get totally squashed by the law of the land.

Matt and I drove up to Albany on a cold and snowy November afternoon in 2010 that reminded my southern bones why I could never live up in these parts. There's something unholy about it snowing before Thanksgiving. We found Scott and Stacy ensconced in their second-floor walkup near downtown to get the lowdown. It was easy to bond over the tribulations of publishing a book, the insane quantity of work, the pitiful pay, the opening up of your life's work to potential desecration by unknown entities in the blogosphere and the strain on one's marriage (fortunately theirs has fared better than my own).

Scott and Stacy got the idea for a physical space for activist groups to come together out of the social justice movement that was picking up steam in the late '90s. The cry was "Another world is possible," but what, exactly, that world would look like was much in question. There was also a lot of myopia on the part of individual groups, each stuck in their own bubble, and they wanted to create the possibility for cross-pollination between those working for egalitarian social causes and those working to implement on-the-ground urban sustainability, feeling strongly that these two causes were ultimately inseparable and that both required a radical rethinking of everyday life. To Scott and Stacy, the word "radical" was very important, more in the sense of its Latin root of "radix" or "root." To create a better world, old methods of thinking like capitalism's claim that pursuing self-interest will lead to endless prosperity had to be extirpated and replaced with a lifestyle that embraced personal responsibility for one's effect on people and the planet. Specifically, they wanted to develop a physical model for what that possible new world might actually look like.

With the windfall of an inheritance, Scott was able to purchase an empty warehouse in east Austin not too far north of the river. By keeping costs low and creating some revenue from the site through residential rents and hosting events, they both hoped to allow socially conscious groups to be able to focus on their own work rather than worrying about the bills each month. After the purchase, they put a call out to local groups to consider moving into the space, with little planning for how to organize the motley collection of misfits that showed up. They referred to the first few years as "The Circus Years," because the first inhabitants were primarily circus freaks and gutter punks with perhaps radical philosophies but whose interests seem to revolve more around music and a generally itinerant lifestyle. There was little private space in the big open warehouse and it wasn't at all clear that the initial vision for the space was coming into fruition. Legally, the space had undergone an initial zoning change to Art and Craft Studio (Limited) with a variance that allowed for one person to maintain permanent residence, but the wording of the law was vague and seemed to permit an unspecified number of guests. Inspectors showed up with some regularity, because the one nearby neighbor was less than thrilled with the commotion and spectacle and repeatedly called the code enforcer.

After some weeding out in the first year or two a more regular presence of perhaps ten to twelve mostly permanent residents added some stability, as did the drafting of some more legitimate groups like Indymedia and Food Not Bombs. Scott and Stacy started work on forming their nonprofit to manage the space, called The Rhizome Collective, and eventually got it approved as a 501-3C nonprofit. It was very apparent that the living situation was untenable for any length of time and that some more private dwellings were vital to the long-term survival of the space. With this and the idea of earning residential rents in mind, individuals began constructing rooms on the roof of the building, using mostly salvaged materials. Not well-versed in managing such a sprawling organization, Rhizome made a tactical error in initially failing to separate out the residential meetings from the organizational meetings, resulting in non-residents interested in helping to move the collective forward having to listen to hour-long discussions about dirty dishes.

At the heart of what Rhizome wanted to accomplish was to have displays and workshops involving ecological tools and technologies under the same roof. Over the first half-decade of their existence, they tore up the asphalt in their third of an acre courtyard space, bringing in tons of organic waste material from around the city to compost and build the soil so they could plant an orchard and other gardens. They built a greywater filtration system, complete with ponds, and installed composting toilets in the warehouse. They raised chickens and other fowl, cultivated mushrooms, built a small wind turbine, installed solar heating and were one of the first places to take advantage of Austin's excellent solar incentives, putting in a 4.8 kilowatt grid-tied

PV system. With these systems installed, Rhizome was able to flesh out their workshop series in a holistic way, which they called R.U.S.T, for Radical Urban Sustainability Training.

During this time, Rhizome was grappling with its supposedly collective nature. Scott and Stacy maintained ownership, and there was no process, formal or informal, for the collective to buy them out and make it a truly egalitarian space. The Rhizome project required a relatively high initial infrastructure investment, and the others involved had few resources to draw from to potentially buy into it. By 2006, Scott and Stacy were the only original members left and Stacy was pregnant. What would it be like to have a small infant in a space where bands sometimes played into the wee hours of the morning? Both of their families were up in New York State. They started spending more

A constructed wetland built with discarded bathtubs at the former Rhizome Collective in Austin, Texas, used to purify wastewater from the washing machine.

Credit: Scott Kellogg and Stacy Pettigrew

time up in Albany, hoping that others would be motivated to take over more of a leadership role as their family grew. Starting a family is one of the most vexing issues that many living on the cutting edge of sustainability face. The trappings of parenthood are enormous, and feeling like you're depriving your child of a "normal" existence can shake many people to their core. Many activists, including myself so far, sidestep this issue by not having any. But on a fundamental level this misses the point, since if you can't be sustainable *with* children, then humanity is *de facto* unsustainable. It was certainly interesting to get Scott and Stacy's perspective on this, and it doesn't seem like a coincidence that the years during which they gave birth to their two children corresponded with a turn to a much more law-abiding, and ultimately much slower, method of activism...but more on that in a bit. It's also interesting to note another phenomenon exemplified here: Founder's Syndrome. It's often the case that individuals who have the vision and creative drive to create or change the system don't possess the patience or organizational wherewithal to lead once it gets off the ground. The political structure of Rhizome had always been ad hoc. Without formal bylaws, elections and a transparent process for moving towards collective ownership, the group began to flounder with Scott and Stacy's prolonged absences.

Meanwhile, the group had stumbled across the chance to obtain ownership of a ten-acre parcel of land on the other side of the Colorado River. The place was a dump, literally, and was classified as a brownfield site. The city was interested in cleaning it up and doing something constructive, especially since the site butted up against 350 additional acres of protected woodlands. The site seemed like a perfect potential example of bioremediation, turning a disgusting disused industrial space into an urban ecological center. With a grant from the city, Rhizome spent the next two years tackling the cleanup. Much of the waste was construction debris, and they sold the rebar for scrap, recycled the empty glass bottles, chipped the old framing lumber for paths and threw away the moldy carpet and other crap that couldn't be reused or recycled. The project won them accolades from public officials and national press in *Time* magazine. The goal was to restore the site to greenspace and turn it into an ecological educational park. With that in mind, they managed to get the first composting toilet approved in the city of Austin as the first public infrastructure at the site.

In 2008, Rhizome ran into a brick wall. The group had watched nervously as the behemoth of gentrification marched eastward towards them. Austin was booming and condo developments were springing up all over town. East Austin was going from being a live-and-let-live, mostly Hispanic barrio to a developer's wet dream. The folks at Rhizome were conflicted about this: while they opposed the gentrification on principle, they knew they were complicit for bringing an artistic and green feel to the neighborhood. Essentially, they were making the neighborhood feel safe for mostly white yuppies. I understood their dilemma, since I also bought and fixed up a home in a mostly Hispanic neighborhood in Durham, and I've watched over the last five years as my neighborhood has slowly tipped towards gentrification. I have no answers for this. It was where I could afford to buy a home, but I don't doubt that my whiteness and greenness have contributed somewhat to the process. To me, it shows that you can never do the exact right thing all the time. Your actions will have unintended consequences, but I also don't believe you can allow fear of these to keep you from doing what you think is mostly right.

A building inspector showed up in response to one of the routine complaints from their neighbor about the legality of their living situation. Baffled by what he saw, he called in his supervisor. It seems that the code department in Austin had undergone a profound shift, hiring many more inspectors and shutting down several other like-minded groups in other marginal spaces. The chief inspector came in and starting asking Scott tough questions about the plumbing and electrical modifications. Scott admitted to me that he dissembled at this point, basically lying and saying that the upgrades had occurred before he purchased the property, hoping against hope that the chief inspector would allow the building to remain grandfathered in. But the inspector knew that the new wiring hadn't been manufactured until 2003, and Scott and Stacy had owned the building since 1999.

On most levels, there's no point in playing a game of "What if?" but I couldn't help but remember my own experience with my inspector back in 2004, and how important that initial truthfulness on my part had been in establishing a working relationship that eventually allowed us to make our cob home legal. The chief inspector made out a long and very vague list about the codes in noncompliance, everything from the plumbing and electrical to the entire second story filled with apartments. He told Scott that the premises had to vacated immediately and that he had to pull permits to upgrade the entire building within 14 days, or he would face a $35,000 a day fine and criminal charges.

With the renters kicked out, Rhizome had no income, and estimates from contractors put the work in the range of $200,000 or more. Scott went before city council to try and broker some kind of compromise that would allow them to stay in the building and make the necessary modifications over a longer period of time. After all, just two years previously they had completed the brownfield restoration and brought national recognition to Austin as a bastion of ecological forwardness. All they got was an extension of the existing terms from 14 to 30 days. They had no choice but to sell the building. At this juncture, other members of the collective wanted to hole up in the building and fight for it, but there was no collective ownership, and the fines and criminal charges would have fallen on Scott's shoulders as the primary owner. Rhizome had come to an end.

Scott and Stacy have since moved to Albany permanently and are working on a new space called Radix. Perhaps symptomatic of their now completely aboveboard approach, they've changed the name Radical Urban Sustainability Training to Regenerative Urban Sustainability Training. They have purchased a half-acre open field near downtown Albany and are finally breaking ground on a greenhouse at the site, after two years of filing paperwork and obtaining permits. There's no doubt that the scope of the new project will be substantially more focused, and less holistic, than the Rhizome collective in Austin. To be aboveboard, before they could begin they had to first acquire a use variance, then get a site plan approval signed off on by architects and engineers and obtain permission from the city clerk to have livestock. At the same time, they feel this allows for more focus, something that was sorely lacking at Rhizome.

Shutting down Rhizome was a major setback for urban sustainability, and in my opinion the city of Austin should be ashamed for not trying harder to work with this obviously well-intentioned and mostly popular group to figure out how to make them legitimate. But that's the nature of the game. Nobody says that when you ask forgiveness it's going to be granted. If your convictions and sense of personal responsibility are strong enough, you have no choice but to do what you think is right to retain your integrity. But that doesn't mean you won't be squashed like a bug if the place you decided to make your stand would make one hell of a condo development. The housing crash later in 2008 stopped that from happening, at least for now, so the old Rhizome building in Austin sits vacant.

Filling up with biodiesel from a passive-solar cob greenhouse in Pittsboro, North Carolina.

Credit: Tami Schwerin

It may have been the case that Rhizome reached too far too fast. By adopting an holistic view of the broad range of changes that needed to be made, they felt compelled to tackle a number of unsustainable activities all at once. Combined with a lack of financial resources once the building was purchased, this meant they ended up in violation of a number of laws and statutes. Where officials can make concessions on one or two points without feeling their authority is ultimately threatened, allowing too blatant a thwarting of too many laws is liable to wound the pride of public officials who, to give them the benefit of the doubt, feel they are obliged to enforce the law as it is if there's going to be any hope of equality and justice. But I have been fortunate to witness a different and ultimately more successful way to challenge outmoded laws during my involvement with and visits to the town of Pittsboro, North Carolina, over the last six years or so. In 2005 I was still in the throes of a peak oil freak out; I was sure of the imminent collapse of our consumerist industrial civilization when I became involved in building a passive solar cob greenhouse for the Piedmont Biofuels cooperative.

I had a deep skepticism of biofuels then that I retain to this day. On a fundamental level I feel like we're burning up our soil for the sake of maintaining our convenient yet ultimately suicidal addiction to the automobile. But during my initial visits to the small co-op six miles outside the small burg of Pittsboro, I was infected with the can-do optimism and endless experimentation that the wonderful folks exhibited there. At that time the co-op was in the process of blossoming out from a ragtag operation in a decaying trailer to a much larger and professional facility a few miles away, retrofitting an abandoned military building, no less. One of the founders and ideological captains of this enterprise is Lyle Estill, a broad thinker, activist and author of soon-to-be-published books like *Biodiesel Power* and *Small is Possible*, and flat-out wacky dresser. Lyle was in the habit of wearing a top hat, baggy floral pants and a variety of gaudy jackets that let anyone within a 50-mile radius know he did not take himself too seriously. But damn did that dude stay busy. Lyle had convinced me, like he has convinced many others, to donate a great deal of my spare time to this enterprise.

I was leading Sunday workshops building the passive solar cob green-house, which was needed to keep the biodiesel warm in the winter since at temperatures near freezing it gels and becomes unpumpable. During a break from this strenuous endeavor, I accompanied several others on a tour of the new facility. Lyle was becoming familiar with my skepticism, but battled it relentlessly with his bottomless well-spring of optimism. After the tour he listened for a minute or two to some of my pointed questions about the sustainability of biodiesel and replied, "Stephen, this is all just a big thought experiment. We don't know what the answers are. We do know that the way things are isn't working, and that sourcing our fuels locally with potentially renewable energy is a lot better than burning fossil fuels." He had me there. Whereas I had been in a reductionist frame of mind that sought to leapfrog to a theoretically sustainable endpoint with no fossil fuels or harm to the environment, Lyle was much more flexible and willing to accept incremental improvements as long as things were moving in the right direction. The perfect is the enemy of the good, as I have always known but frequently forget.

Over the years I've talked with Lyle many times, and we've become good friends. The subject of legality has come up with regularity since, obviously, it's one of my pet subjects. As the energy from Piedmont Biofuels has helped spawn other regenerative enterprises around its periphery like an organic farm, a grocery co-op and a regional currency, there have been never-ending opportunities for run-ins with antiquated laws. From greywater recycling to dealing with nontoxic byproducts getting labelled toxic waste to receiving donations from only "accredited investors" — if there's an activity two people engage in, somewhere at some time a law was written about it that's still on the books.

To sell a gallon of biodiesel, for example, you can't just make a simple transaction based on the trust between the two parties involved. It has to be metered, and obtaining an official meter requires a big chunk of change that is going to add a heavy fixed cost to an operation that might start out selling only a few hundred gallons a week. "When is a gallon a gallon?" Lyle asked. Only when a public official says so. Numerous rules and regulations surround fuel, as you can imagine for a product so essential to most of our daily lives. They are also arcane and pretty boring, so I won't take up your time going into the nitty gritty of any of them. Suffice it to say that starting out in any of these endeavors requires a bit of stealth and a healthy disregard for the law of the land. Enforcers of the law are usually as apt to enforce a law when it involves just a small number of people as when it involves megacorporations whose modus operandi is ever-increasing profits at the expense of everything else. But Lyle and the many other hardworking folks at Piedmont Biofuels and around Pittsboro have adopted an informal philosophy that prizes expediency and a mild disregard for the law in the early phases of a given project while the kinks are worked out, then shifts gears to a more active involvement with officialdom as the size of the project grows and becomes more public. They have often found that the cooperative structure of their enterprises helps greatly in this regard, since inspectors and their ilk seem much less interested in strict enforcement among equal owners of an organization. Since scale-appropriate regulation is so often nonexistent, they achieve the same effect through stealth, organizational structure and a healthy skepticism of the written regulations. By adopting this pragmatic approach and combining it with optimism and relentless hard work, they have made their community a paragon of exploratory sustainability, the letter of the law be damned.

Conclusion

W E WOKE UP IN THIS WORLD that cannot be sustained. What a heavy realization that is. There's so much good in our lives and our world, from the joy of being with our friends and family to the flourishing of science and the spread of democracy and racial equality over the last several centuries. At the same time expectations and accepted behavior have formed around a consumerist and corporate way of life that profoundly jeopardizes our very home.

At this critical turning point we need to be as flexible and exploratory as possible, yet the momentum of the juggernaut of unquestioning conformity embedded in our laws and mores has created a rigidity that impedes us. We pride ourselves on our ability to adapt and our love of the pioneer and small businessperson, yet we walk around in a trance while those who struggle against the forces that would destroy us face endless red tape, detrimental laws and ridicule.

I couldn't help but see some synchronicity in Dabl's *Iron Teaching Rocks How to Rust* and the Rhizome's R.U.S.T. workshops. Iron, though it's forged from fire and provides the structural strength of so much of our civilization's infrastructure, is nevertheless part of a larger mineral cycle that mimics so many other cycles on our planet. Iron is dispersed by another vital cycle of water and rain, and returns to the soil, just like all of our "waste" does. To maintain our civilization, we have to re-accumulate iron through fire and energy, both of these part of their own integrated cycles, in the same way that plants recycle their needed nutrients from the soil through capturing solar energy in their leaves and the capillary action of their roots. If rocks are the authority and structure of our laws, the plant's stem, then the fluid nature of iron needs to teach rocks how to become flexible and adapt. Rigidity in our beliefs and behaviors is the greatest threat to our own survival and the survival of all that we've come to love in civilization. We need to learn to bend in order not to break.

When I asked Scott Kellogg if he thought there was any way Rhizome would have happened if it had tried to be legit from the start, he said, "No way." Their holistic approach was too encompassing, and would have required too many variances to too many laws, meaning way too much time and money, to get off the ground. Ultimately, the question we have to ask is if our systems of politics and economy are flexible enough to become sustainable, because if they aren't, we have to figure out how to get rid of them and replace them with systems that can be.

In *Letters to a Young Poet*, Rainer Maria Rilke gives some famous advice to the young novice, just out of adolescence, who has written him with his doubts and worries: in times of great change you don't get to know the answers, all you can do is *live the questions*. This is a personal struggle I've gone through myself. I've always wanted to have a ready answer, partly, I think, just so I wouldn't go crazy with so much uncertainty. But nothing in life is ever settled, especially in the days we now live in. What a noble pursuit to dive into the seeming abyss of ignorance and misunderstanding and try to make sense and find an answer for what appears unknowable or even impossible. It's amazing to be engaged in such a pursuit, with new doorways forever opening that you could never have foreseen one or two rooms back, and realize that the path you are on is a meaningful life, even if you never get to the end. Things will get better, in increments, if we *do*, and if we live the questions that now seem so daunting and overwhelming. We are all fighting for life, and the only constant of the cycle of life is change.

Index

Page numbers in *italics* indicate photographs.

If you have enjoyed *Tales from the Sustainability Underground,*
you might also enjoy other

BOOKS TO BUILD A NEW SOCIETY

Our b̶... ...e solutions for people who want to
... ... ̶e. We specialize in:

Sustainable Living · Green Building · Peak Oil
Renewable Energy · Environment & Economy
Natural Building & Appropriate Technology
Progressive Leadership · Resistance and Community
Educational & Parenting Resources

New Society Publishers

ENVIRONMENTAL BENEFITS STATEMENT

New Society Publishers has chosen to produce this book on recycled paper made
with **100% post consumer waste,** processed chlorine free, and old growth free.
For every 5,000 books printed, New Society saves the following resources:[1]

22	Trees
1,976	Pounds of Solid Waste
2,174	Gallons of Water
2,836	Kilowatt Hours of Electricity
3,592	Pounds of Greenhouse Gases
15	Pounds of HAPs, VOCs, and AOX Combined
5	Cubic Yards of Landfill Space

---

[1]Environmental benefits are calculated based on research done by the Environmental Defense
Fund and other members of the Paper Task Force who study the environmental impacts of the
paper industry.

For a full list of NSP's titles, please call 1-800-567-6772 *or check out our website* at:

www.newsociety.com

NEW SOCIETY PUBLISHERS

About the Author

STEPHEN HREN takes a holistic view towards how our lives need to be rearranged to create a sustainable and empowering existence. He has rehabbed homes to wean them from fossil fuels, built an off-grid house out of cob, installed solar air heating equipment, worked to establish a worker- and community-owned cooperative grocery, been a member of an edible landscaping collective, coauthored two books on renewable energy and written articles for *Homepower* and *Backwoods* magazines, and is currently employed at a restaurant in downtown Durham focusing on local foods. Visit his website www.earthonaut.net to see more and read more, including more photos and video of folks profiled in this book. Or send him an email and tell him your crazy sustainable adventure at stephenhren@gmail.com.